STANISLAVSKI AND THE ACTOR

Westminster Kingsway College

DEP 1

STANISLAVSKI AND THE ACTOR

Jean Benedetti

Routledge
Taylor & Francis Group

LONDON AND NEW YORK

First published by Methuen in Great Britain in 1998

Published in the USA by
Routledge
Taylor & Francis Group
711 Third Avenue
New York, NY 10017

ISBN 0 87830 090 2

A CIP catalogue record for this book
is available from the British Library
and from the Library of Congress

Methuen, an imprint of Random House UK Limited
20 Vauxhall Bridge Road, London SW1V 2SA

Typeset by MATS, Southend-on-Sea, Essex

CONTENTS

ACKNOWLEDGEMENTS

My sincere and grateful thanks are due to Martin Kurtén, Stanislavski's translator into Swedish, who brought his considerable expertise to bear on an early draft and made many invaluable suggestions which have been incorporated into the final text.

I am also grateful to Professor S. Nikulin and Art Publishers, Moscow for kind permission to use and translate material from Novitskaya's book, *Uroki Vdoxnovenija* (Iskusstvo, Moscow, 1984) and from the Stanislavski transcripts contained in *Stanislavskij Repetiruet*, (Iskusstvo, Moscow, 1987).

All translations of texts, unless otherwise indicated, are my own.

The quotation from Stanislavski's production plan for *Othello*, is taken from *Rezhisiorskij Plan 'Otello'*, Iskusstvo, Moscow, 1945.

Finally, my thanks, as ever, to Michael Earley, my publisher, for his sympathetic and perceptive guidance and advice in shaping the book and bringing it to its final form.

INTRODUCTION

Konstantin Stanislavski is the most significant and most frequently quoted figure in the history of actor training. He is also the most consistently and widely misunderstood. By 1980, after spending ten years devising and teaching acting courses based on the Stanislavski 'system' at Rose Bruford College in England, and seeing work elsewhere, both in the UK and abroad, I had become aware of the confusion that existed as to what precisely the 'system' was. It was often identified either with a primitive kind of 'naturalism' or with Lee Strasberg's Method.

It was then that I started to write *Stanislavski: An Introduction* (Methuen, 1982), in an attempt to provide students with an account of the origins of the 'system' and a guide to reading Stanislavski's published works. I had to rely at that time on existing English-language translations of these books, unsatisfactory and misleading though they sometimes were because of heavy cuts. *An Actor Prepares,* for example, is only about half the length of Stanislavski's original. But these were the only texts available for students to buy and there seemed no prospect, for copyright reasons, of producing much-needed new translations. I followed the *Introduction* with *Stanislavski: A Biography* (Methuen, 1990) in which I tried to chart the long and often painful path Stanislavski followed in order to understand the nature of the art to which he had devoted his life.

My continuing work at my own college, and as consultant and examiner to other institutions, together with my fourteen-year term as President of the Theatre Education Committee of the International Theatre Institute (UNESCO) convinced me of the absolute necessity of providing new translations that would make available what Stanislavski had actually written. My view was shared internationally by colleagues equally anxious to produce versions in their own languages. I recalled that as early as 1953, Bertolt Brecht, realising the inadequacy of his own knowledge, had called for complete translations of Stanislavski's work so that he could clear up his own confusions.

In the early 1990s the copyright problems surrounding Stanislavski's works were resolved, and long-overdue work could start on new versions of *An Actor's Work on Himself, Parts One and Two (Rabota Aktiora nad Soboj)* and *An Actor's Work on a Role (Rabota Aktiora nad Rolju)* which had appeared in English as *An Actor Prepares* (1936), *Building A Character* (1950) and *Creating a Role* (1961). It seemed that students and tutors would at last have available the teaching material they needed. In the event, however, the project raised a number of major problems.

First, Stanislavski was not a natural writer. His most accessible and entertaining book, *My Life in Art*, was dictated to his secretary and so has all the ease of his conversational style. But when he sat down to write about his methods, in his effort to be absolutely clear he relentlessly crossed all the 't's and dotted all the 'i's, thus achieving the very opposite of what he intended. His style became convoluted, verbose and confusing. There are passages which almost defy comprehension, let alone translation. You can see what he means but the words get in the way. Many specialists felt that by using the fictional form of an imaginary student's diary and by disguising himself as Tortsov, Stanislavski had merely added to his problems – and ours. Some Russian teachers admitted to me that they had never read *An Actor's Work on Himself*. But these were private admissions. No one wanted or, perhaps, dared to admit in public that Stanislavski's books were a problem. They were, after all, supposed to be the collective Bible of acting.

By the time the Soviet authorities began to issue the eight-volume *Collected Works* in the 1950s, Stanislavski had long been established in the Stalinist pantheon as a cult figure beyond criticism. His writings had to be treated with reverence and awe. If, in the United States, Stanislavski had suffered from savage and often inept editing, in the USSR he suffered from no editing at all. Yet he himself always recognised his need for editorial advice and relied on friends and associates to help him, though they were often driven to despair by his constant revisions and additions after they had introduced a measure of order into his drafts.

Second, there was the problem of Stanislavski's terminology, the special set of terms he devised for the main elements of the 'system', a problem compounded by the fact that Stanislavski never hesitated to change terms, or use different terms in different situations in the same period of his life. The terminology he used when teaching was not always the terminology he used in his published books or in his drafts. Sometimes he would use alternative terms in two different classes. The 'system' was not about words but about method. In *An Actor's Work on Himself,* Stanislavski/Tortsov rather impatiently tells a student that provided he understands the nature of the activity he is engaged in, it doesn't matter what name he gives it.

While Stanislavski wanted his ideas to be scientifically valid, he did not want to create an abstract jargon so obscure and complicated that it would block an actor's creative processes or become an end in itself. He envied musicians who had a set of words indicating tempo, rhythm and expression that provided a quick, universal way of communicating. Actors and directors needed a similar shorthand which they could use when entering into lengthy, abstract discussions.

To create an equivalent to musical terms, Stanislavski tried to use ordinary, everyday words, occasionally shaping their meaning to suit his purpose. The difficulty is that words that are ordinary in Russian are not always ordinary or idiomatic when translated into other languages. The problems all translators experience in trying to find workable equivalents were the subject of a number of international seminars in the late 1980s but they have still not been completely resolved. Where you find two or three Stanislavski specialists together, you will find a heated debate about words. But there is general agreement on one fundamental principle: whatever terms we use in translation, we must create an easy, simple, unpretentious working vocabulary to be used in the classroom and the rehearsal room.

This automatically precludes some of the alternative acting and performance vocabularies that have been developed over recent years to discuss the actor's process and performance.

These are rooted in anthropology, sociology and semiology and whatever their undoubted intellectual or theoretical merits, they belong to the social sciences; they are the language of commentary and critical analysis, not of creative rehearsal work. None of them would help a student get through the most elementary acting exercise. Actors in rehearsal do not explore concepts, or work on the basis of a theory of performance. They are concerned with getting *into* the script, not viewing it from the outside. 'Art ends where philosophy begins,' Stanislavski stated. The problem of finding usable equivalents, therefore, goes on. Stanislavski always stressed the provisional nature of his findings, hence his usage of the 'system' with a small 's' and in quotes, never System, with a capital 'S' that suggested a closed and rigid theory. The truth of the matter might be constant but our formulation of it, and the words we use to describe it, change.

Third, even supposing we manage to solve the problems of translation, there would still be another formidable barrier for modern readers. Reluctant though we may be to admit it, Stanislavski's books are now historic documents. He was born in 1863; his outlook and style belong to the nineteenth century. His books are of their time and any translation has to take that into account and reflect in its style the very special period flavour of the originals. Reading and studying them closely over many years, I have become increasingly aware of the mental effort that has to be made to place them within their historical context, without which they cannot genuinely make sense. The principles of the 'system' may be constant, but the manner and style in which they are expressed is conditioned by time and place. Stanislavski recognised this when, in the 1938 preface to *An Actor's Work on Himself, Part One,* he acknowledged that much of the material and most of the examples he used were twenty-five years old, dating from the old Russia before the Revolution. Regrettably, there was no time to update them.

Fourth, the texts that have come down to us are not complete. They are fragments of a grand design which Stanislavski outlined in a letter to his secretary at the end of 1930. He envisaged a sequence of seven books. The first of these was the Russian edition of *My Life in Art* published in 1926 (still not satisfactorily translated into English). This was to be followed by books on acting, directing and opera. *An Actor's Work on Himself* was originally conceived as a single volume covering both the mental and physical aspects of an actor's technique, but for technical reasons it had to be split into two parts. Stanislavski was not happy about this decision as he feared that if *Part One* appeared alone it would convey a false impression of 'ultra-naturalism', which has indeed proved to be the case. Had *Part One* not appeared separately, however, we might never have had another completed book after *My Life in Art.*

An Actor's Work on Himself, Part One was published in September 1938, only a few weeks after Stanislavski's death, but it was already out of date since he had drafted a number of passages for insertion into future editions. In the preface he also regretted that he had not had time to write a handbook of exercises that would set out day-to-day, classroom work in greater detail and could be used in parallel.

One or two chapters of *Part Two* were completed by his death, but the rest were in note or draft form. The new Russian edition collates the material more effectively but the text is still provisional.

An Actor's Work on Himself on a Role was never even started. The book, as we have it, is 'material for a book', a compilation of articles and drafts drawn from various periods of Stanislavski's life. Even the new revised version of 1991 is simply an expansion of earlier editions with the addition of much new material.

At Stanislavski's death, therefore, all that was left of his grand design was *My Life in Art* (1926), one volume on acting still being revised, a series of drafts and some titles. Much of the material was not published until the 1950s.

Unfinished, provisional though they are, these books are still essential documents which we must have complete, if we are to understand Stanislavski's mind and thinking and the origins of the 'system'. Anyone interested in Stanislavski must read them. But without the manual of exercises that should have accompanied them, they do not provide, for the strict purposes of training, a clear practical guide to detailed, daily classroom work over three or four years' study. They only provide a set of principles, strategies, guidelines, with a small number of acting exercises and improvisations, some of which are repeated three or four times over, to illustrate the processes.

What then do we do in the classroom? How, at the end of the twentieth century, and sixty years after Stanislavski's death, are we to study the 'system'? How are we, teachers and acting students, to achieve a clear view of what it is, to get the 'inside' view as it were, that enables us to master our craft? If not the books, then what?

The answer is to be found elsewhere, in the work of the Opera-Dramatic Studio where from mid-1935, when he was seventy-two and very ill, until a few weeks before his death in August 1938, Stanislavski, with a group of assistants, gave a complete course in the 'system'. It was his desperate response to the realisation that he would never complete his books, his final attempt to pass on his ideas as a coherent whole. The four years of the course covered the same ground as Stanislavski's three projected books on the actor's work.

In June 1935, eleven hand-picked young actors and directors gathered at Stanislavski's apartment at 6 Leontievski Lane (now Stanislavski Lane). They were to be his assistants. As pupils of his sister, Zinaïda, they had a basic knowledge of the 'system'. During the summer they auditioned some 3,500 students of whom twenty were selected for the drama section. Then, in the autumn, Stanislavski took them through the elements of the 'system' again and demonstrated his rehearsal method. The first class with students took place on 15 November 1935.

Stanislavski did not write down what he taught but his assistants and students made extensive notes while his own sessions were taken down, like all his work, in shorthand. We thus have a record of the 'system' as taught in the classroom, simply, directly, practically, not, as in *An Actor's Work on Himself*, in the form of a diary kept by an imaginary student.

The work of the Opera-Dramatic Studio is Stanislavski's true testament. This legacy was handed down from teacher to teacher in major theatre schools, and a tradition of training was created long before a full edition of his works was published.

This body of practice, therefore, essentially remained the preserve of Stanislavski's disciples and their successors. Outside Russia it was known only to a handful of specialists who managed to observe class work at first hand.

In 1984, however, Irina Novitskaya, who had been one of Stanislavski's assistants at the Studio, published a personal account of its foundation and its work in her book, *Uroki Vdoxnovenija* which she based on notes taken by herself and her colleagues.

Having used it regularly as a source of material for my own teaching, my first inclination was to translate and perhaps edit Novitskaya's book and so provide a clear, authentic account of the 'system' as taught by Stanislavski. It seemed the simplest solution to our problems. But when I came to look at it more closely, not as an occasional source of information, but as a complete whole, I realised that it is no more immediately accessible to a young reader than Stanislavski's own works. It is a mixture of personal reminiscences, accounts of the work which she developed after Stanislavski's death, and her own explanations of the elements of the 'system' with liberal quotations from Stanislavski's works. It is as much an act of homage to a beloved teacher as a definition of principles. The very title, *Inspiring Lessons,* is indicative of the tone.

At its core, however, are sets of exercises and improvisations, examples of student work, Stanislavski's outline of his rehearsal method with examples of its practical application, and verbatim accounts of his own rehearsal classes. These make up the hard information which we need for our daily work.

I decided, therefore, that I would use this factual, practical core of Novitskaya's book as the centre of my own, but that all exposition of the elements of the 'system' and any explanation of the rationale of Stanislavski's rehearsal method would be mine, based on my own previous research and the teaching I had done at all levels, both in the UK and elsewhere, from secondary to post-graduate. That experience had indicated the path I should take. Students and teachers required an explanation of Stanislavski's work clearly expressed in the vocabulary of our own time. I had to modernise.

I felt this modernisation was legitimate. Stanislavski always insisted that his work had to be useful and that it should be extended and developed. He also recognised that different countries and different cultures would need to adapt the 'system' to their own requirements. The one condition he laid down was that its basic principles, which he believed to be rooted in human biology, should be respected. I have accepted that invitation and that limitation. Whatever the degree of modernisation, it is a matter of presentation, not substance. *Stanislavski and the Actor* strictly respects the sequence of study that Stanislavski laid down both for the 'system' and for the rehearsal process.

Stanislavski hoped that eventually science would provide a clear set of terms to replace his own home-grown vocabulary. At the time he was writing, the right kind of scientific research did not exist. But in the sixty years that have passed since his death there have been significant developments in the study of memory, linguistics, non-verbal communication and reception theory, much of which has entered common parlance. We all talk freely now about 'body language', but it is a term that has only been current for about twenty-five years. I have used such simple, basic modern concepts to explain the elements of the 'system' to a readership at home in the new scientific world.

I have also taken account of the gulf between the oppressive, technically backward Soviet Union of the 1930s and the modern technological society of the millennium. Stanislavski always insisted that all exercises should be closely related to students' direct, day-to-day experience. I have accordingly updated some of the exercises.

One further word of explanation is essential. Stanislavski's rehearsal method came to be known by his successors as the 'Method of Physical Action'. This is a term that has caused much confusion. Many assume it means that acting is reduced only to what actors do physically on stage, or that it is concerned with problems of stage movement.

Some Russian teachers have preferred the term, the Method of Analysis through Physical Action. This is more accurate.

What Stanislavski wanted to provide was a method for *actors* to explore the play, the events as they unfold, in terms of what they would *do* in the various situations the author provided, using exercises and improvisations. It is active analysis on the rehearsal-room floor, as opposed to the reflective, formal analysis that takes place in the study; it first asks what happens, rather than what the dramaturgical structure is. For Stanislavski, the Method of Physical Action was the most effective way for actors initially to get into the play; it provided the means to liberate their imagination and their creative forces. Physical action is the foundation on which the entire emotional, mental and philosophical superstructure of the ultimate performance is built.

Jean Benedetti
Les Fontenelles
August 1997

HOW TO USE THIS BOOK

Stanislavski and the Actor is intended to be a free-standing, contemporary manual that can be used in class without reference to other works. In some sense it represents the manual that Stanislavski wanted, but did not have time, to write.

While it is intended principally for young actors in training and their teachers, I hope that it may be useful to others who are interested in the art of acting. Those who are concerned with the comparative study of acting methods may find Part One especially relevant, while those whose concern is the rehearsal process may be more interested in Parts Three and Four. Some teachers and students may wish to concentrate on Part Two. The four parts can, in fact, be read in the order that best suits the reader's needs.

The scheme of the book is as follows:

Part One: My own outline of the basic principles underlying the Method of Physical Action, expressed in terms of contemporary knowledge.

Part Two: An examination of the elements of the 'system' and actor training. Each section begins with my own explanation of the subject matter and is followed by sets of exercises, most of which are taken from Novitskaya, and some of which I have modified to meet the contemporary situation. Other exercises I have invented, using the Stanislavski exercises as a model. This is particularly true of those concerning language and speech patterns. Stanislavski was fond of quoting examples from Russian literature, plays and books unfamiliar to non-Russian readers. These have been replaced with parallel examples from English literature. Descriptions of work by the students at the Studio are clearly marked '*Studio Notes*'. This section reconstructs the handbook Stanislavski wanted to write.

Part Three: The Method of Physical Action in rehearsal. This includes a model of the rehearsal process formulated on the basis of Stanislavski's many drafts and notes, examples of the way in which the members of the Studio under Stanislavski's supervision applied it, and my own suggestions as to how we might use it today, concentrating on *Hamlet*. This section can, with the one that follows, in some small way stand in for the missing *An Actor's Work on a Role*.

Part Four: Edited transcripts of Stanislavski's rehearsal work or master classes on *Hamlet* with the Studio members. My contribution here has been to collate the differing accounts of the same class provided by student notes and the verbatim transcripts.

Appendices: These contain a discussion of Stanislavski's varying use of terminology and an Index of key terms which appear in bold print throughout the book so that readers may cross refer from one part to another.

A short biographical note follows this introduction.

STANISLAVSKI:
A BIOGRAPHICAL NOTE

Konstantin Sergeevich Alekseev (Stanislavski) was born in 1863 into a family of rich textile manufacturers. The Alekseev factories had the monopoly on manufacture of all gold and silver thread throughout the Russian Empire. Stanislavski's mother was the daughter of a French actress, who had made her name in Petersburg.

The family passion was the theatre, everything from the circus to the Bolshoi Opera. As in most well-to-do households, amateur theatricals were part of family life. In 1877, Stanislavski's father transformed a barn at his country estate near Moscow into a small theatre. It was here that Stanislavski confronted an audience other than his own relatives for the first time. Later, one of the larger rooms of the Alekseev town house was also turned into a theatre. Stanislavski and his brothers and sisters created the Alekseev Circle, which staged, among other things, the Russian première of Gilbert and Sullivan's *Mikado*. The productions often evoked favourable critical comment in the press.

The experience of appearing on a public stage raised many questions in Stanislavski's mind. He was struck by the contrast between the ease and relaxation of the great actors, both Russian and foreign, which he saw at the imperial Maly Theatre, and his own clumsy efforts. He could not understand his inability to judge the quality of his own acting, or to know when he was acting well. At fourteen, he began to keep a notebook in which he analysed his problems. He kept such a notebook regularly throughout his life until his death at the age of seventy-five in 1938.

Stanislavski made great efforts to improve his technique as an actor. Like his brothers and sisters he had been taught dance by members of the Bolshoi Theatre, gymnastics and singing. He could ride and fence. He trained himself as far as he could and took further singing lessons from Fyodor Komissarzhevski of the Bolshoi Opera. He enrolled at a drama school when he was twenty-one but only stayed two weeks because all he was being taught was how to imitate older actors' tricks. What no one seemed able to define for him was the nature of the acting process. He felt that there had to be, as he wrote in his diary for April 1885, a 'grammar' of acting.

In 1887, Stanislavski founded the Society of Art and Literature, a semi-professional company which nonetheless achieved the highest standards. This provided him with the opportunity to work with directors who had been trained in the realistic school of acting for which the Maly had once been famous. He was systematically stripped of all his clichés, his false theatrical tricks and made to base his acting on the observation of real life, on actual, not theatrical behaviour. At the same time he was developing his skills as a director.

In 1897, Stanislavski decided to create a professional company. He was, by this time, one of the leading actors and directors of his generation and had received a number of invitations to join the Maly. He refused on each occasion. He wanted a new kind of theatre.

While he was making plans for his new company he was contacted by Vladimir Nemirovich-Danchenko, a leading dramatist and critic, who shared many of his ideals. Together, after a marathon eighteen-hour discussion in June 1897, they created the Moscow Art Theatre.

Stanislavski had by then achieved a technical mastery that enabled him to play a wide range of roles. His skill as a director and his ability to find imaginative solutions to problems of staging were unequalled. With Nemirovich-Danchenko he staged plays by Chekhov, Gorki, Hauptmann and Ibsen. The first six years of the Moscow Art Theatre were a period of intense creativity.

Cracks began to appear in the relationship between Stanislavski and Nemirovich-Danchenko in 1905 and by 1906 Stanislavski was in a state of personal crisis. Not only could he not agree with Nemirovich-Danchenko on the future policy of the theatre, he had stopped feeling creative as an actor. He felt that he had become mechanical, an empty shell, relying on external technique but with no real inner feeling, and that without feeling an actor had nothing essential to communicate to an audience. It was out of this crisis that the 'system' was born.

Stanislavski had always been a master of outer action and had used actions both in his own performances and in the staging he provided for other actors in his early production plans to stimulate the emotions. He could control the externals, the moves, the spatial relationships; he could use lighting and sound to establish a mood that would help his cast find the right feelings. But how could he control inner action? How could he evoke, shape and organise feelings? How could he take the chance out of the process of acting? He returned to his notion of a 'grammar'. The first draft of that 'grammar', which came to be known as the 'system', was begun in the summer of 1906 based on the material he had amassed in his notebooks. The development and elaboration of the 'system' occupied him for the next thirty-two years of his life and was still not complete by his death in August 1938.

Stanislavski's ideas did not gain immediate acceptance at the Moscow Art Theatre or in the acting profession in general, particularly from those who believed that acting was a matter of 'nature'. Although the 'system' was declared the official working method of the Moscow Art Theatre in 1911, this was no more than an attempt to repair the increasingly poor relationship between Stanislavski and Nemirovich-Danchenko who was, in fact, hostile to many of Stanislavski's ideas. Although Stanislavski had proved the efficacy of the 'system' in two major productions, *A Month in the Country* (1909) and *Hamlet* (1911), he remained very much an isolated figure at the Moscow Art Theatre, having resigned from the board of management in 1908. Stanislavski's endless search for new creative ideas, for new experiment was at odds with his colleagues' desire for stability and their wish to hold on to a formula which had brought them success.

As a result, between 1912 and 1924 Stanislavski created a series of studios where he could teach a younger and more receptive generation. His pupils included Vakhtangov, Michael

Chekhov and Richard Boleslavsky, who were to exercise a considerable influence on the theatre for the next forty years.

After the Revolution, the Moscow Art Theatre came under attack from the far Left as a relic of a bygone era. In the years 1922–24 the theatre was sent on tour to Paris and the United States where Stanislavski's methods made a considerable impact. On his return, Stanislavski found himself in sole charge of the Moscow Art Theatre from 1925 to 1927 and under his direction it was relaunched with a series of brilliant productions ranging from Beaumarchais's *The Marriage of Figaro* to *The Armoured Train 14-69*, which became the model for the new Soviet play, as well as the much more controversial *The Days of the Turbins* adapted from a novel by Bulgakov. The 'system' became a working reality.

In 1928, Stanislavski suffered a major heart attack on stage during the thirtieth anniversary celebrations of the Moscow Art Theatre, which effectively put an end to his career as an actor. It was during his subsequent convalescence in Germany and France that he began seriously drafting *An Actor's Work on Himself*. Since the summer of 1906 he had made innumerable drafts of potential books, trying out various forms including the novel, but had abandoned them all. Although he had given a series of lectures on the 'system' for singers at the Bolshoi Opera Studio between 1919 and 1922, he was convinced that straight exposition of theory did not appeal to actors and that he must find a more entertaining form to engage their interest. He finally settled on that of a diary kept by a student in training, recording his day-to-day experiences. It was during this period abroad that he met Elizabeth Hapgood who, with her husband, Norman, translated and arranged the American publication of his books.

On his return to Russia in 1933, Stanislavski worked exclusively at home, rehearsing actors for new productions, drafting his books and from 1935 working with young actors and directors at the Opera-Dramatic Studio.

He died in August 1938 having only taught three years of the planned four-year course. The work was completed by his assistants, following the guidelines he had laid down.

What does it signify, to write down what is past and done. The system lives in me but it has no shape or form. The system is created in the very act of writing it down. That is why I have to keep changing what I have already written.

Stanislavski, 1936

PART ONE

An Outline of the Method of Physical Action

THE ACTOR'S DILEMMA

I am an actor. My job is to appear to be someone else. But I cannot actually *be* someone else. The only feelings or thoughts or impulses I can have are my own. I cannot actually experience anyone else's emotions any more than I can eat and digest anyone else's meal. If I really believe I am someone else then I am, in Stanislavski's words, a pathological case and need psychiatric help.

As an actor, no matter what my appearance, no matter what my ability to transform myself through costume and make-up, at the centre will always be myself. I have no other resource from which to create a performance but my own life.

So, if I can only be myself, how do I create and present a character whom an audience accepts as a fully rounded, comprehensible human being, but who is not me? How do I move them to laughter or tears? How do I change the way they think and feel about the world they live in?

I do it by using a natural process.

Human beings have an innate sympathy for one another, the capacity to feel for one another. If I see someone close to me in distress, I feel distress. They cry, I cry. We are crying as separate individuals, but our crying is *similar*. This is a mechanism so fundamental I take it for granted. I can also, of course, be critical, pass judgement, feel hostile. But I am not indifferent. People who cannot feel anything towards their fellow humans are considered as somehow deficient and abnormal.

It is precisely this capacity to reflect back, to respond to and judge other people's thoughts and feelings that is at the root of art.†

Stanislavski believed that the actor most likely to affect an audience profoundly is the actor who behaves most like a complete human being, thereby stirring not merely their emotions but their minds as well. His art is based on an understanding of the way we behave in our daily lives, which he then uses when creating a character. If a character's behaviour is similar to our behaviour in life, then it becomes 'human'.

The first step in the creative process, therefore, is to look at the way we behave.

EVERYDAY BEHAVIOUR

Necessity

In life I act out of human **Necessity**.‡ I drink because I am thirsty. I eat because I am hungry. My behaviour is purposeful or, as the child psychologist, Jean Piaget, put it, goal-directed. I have needs and intentions, which I respond to through actions. There is no such thing as unmotivated behaviour, even if my motives are not clear to me. Thinking, too, is purposive. I think *about* something.

I interact with the world about me all the time, accept it or change it.

Feelings

Feelings, emotions, moods, states of mind, Stanislavski realised, arise as a result of that interaction. Emotions are not objects, like chairs or tables or books. Love, hate, envy, greed, anger do

---

† 'Art is based on the fact that one man, hearing or seeing another man's expression of feeling, is capable of experiencing the same feeling as the person expressing it.' Tolstoi, Lev Nikolaevich, *Chto kakoe iskusstvo*, in *Sobranie Sochinenij v Vosm'i Tomax*, t. 8 (Leksika, Moscow, 1996), p. 203. Stanislavski was familiar with this key work, published in 1898.

‡ Key terms appear in bold type throughout the book for cross-reference. A full list appears in Appendix Two.

not exist anywhere. Experiencing an emotion is not like plugging into an electric socket, pressing the switch so that an emotion comes on, like a light bulb. Emotions are states which are produced by activity, they are the result of a process, of actions designed to fulfil an intention.

The Real 'I'

When I speak or do something, my words and actions bear the imprint of my personality. They are not 'objective' or 'neutral', they are part of me, the result of my life experience. What I say is coloured, shaped by who I am. There is a **Real 'I'**. That is what other people perceive. If two different people speak the same words, the effect is different. People read each other's behaviour, their faces, their personality, their body language. They don't merely take in the logical content of what is being said, which only accounts for a small fraction of the total message.

Automatic Reflexes

Most of my actions are automatic, things I do out of habit. Stanislavski believed that some 90 per cent of normal behaviour was automatic. When I walk, for instance, I do not consciously motivate each leg each time I move it. I learned to walk as a baby. I know I can do it, I take it for granted. In life I consciously make decisions, create intentions, but the actions I perform to carry them out are, for the most part, reflex. If I decide to write a letter, I may think consciously about what I am going to say, but my hands will write or type apparently of their own accord, spontaneously. These are what we might call operations, we operate as a machine operates.

Organic Actions

Stanislavski defined the sequences of habitual actions, the operations we perform as **Organic Actions**. By this he meant actions which have their own logic and must be performed in a certain sequence. It is no good, for example, sealing an envelope and putting a stamp on it before I have written the letter. The sequence of actions remains the same whatever the situation, whatever I am feeling, whether the letter is a happy or a sad one.

CREATED BEHAVIOUR

The Dramatic 'I'

Spontaneous thoughts and feelings and reaction to other people's thoughts and feelings are not art. But if I tell a story about something that happened to me, and deliberately try to make my listeners share the feelings that I am reliving as I speak, that is the beginning of the art.† If I act out events which I have not actually experienced but which someone else has described, and try to make the people watching experience what I am experiencing, that is the beginning of acting.

Acting is *created* behaviour, prepared spontaneity, something which looks like life but is, in fact, a selection from life, organised in such a way to make an audience participate in the events being shown.

To do that, I have to create a **Dramatic 'I'** that will look and sound as human as a **Real 'I'**.

How do I get from a **Real 'I'** to a **Dramatic 'I'**?

The Method of Physical Action is designed to solve that problem by making me start from where I am, as a human being, so that I can go to where I want to be as an artist.

It has two fundamental principles:

1. That I can do nothing creatively until I know what happens in the play, what the situations are, what demands they make.
2. That by finding out what happens and deciding what I would do physically in any given situation, and believing in the truth of my actions, I release my creative energies and my natural emotional responses organically, without

† Tolstoi, op. cit., pp. 204–205.

forcing, without falling into familiar acting clichés. In Stanislavski's words I go *through the conscious to the sub-conscious.*

What is this process?

FROM THE REAL 'I' TO THE DRAMATIC 'I': FROM SCRIPT TO PERFORMANCE

The Script

When I am cast in a play I am given a script. What is it? Black marks on a page. If I take a script written in Chinese, Hindi or Egyptian hieroglyphics, I see it for what it is – calligraphy. If I take a script in a foreign language which I know moderately well, I can make out the surface meaning of the words. I know, more or less, what the characters are talking about. If I take a modern script in my own language, I will take in not only the words but see the social reality that lies behind them, a world with which I am familiar, my world.

The script gives us information, a series of suggestions concerning a possible sequence of events in which certain imaginary individuals participate.

The ' events', the 'characters' in a play do not exist in the way real events and real people exist. They will not be seen on the evening news, nor can we interview the people involved. They exist only insofar as I believe they might be true, or might have happened, and create them out of my own resources, physical and mental. The only way in which marks on a page can become a play, a kind of reality, is through my natural capacity for make-believe. The essential factor is *belief.* If I believe something to be true and follow the consequences of that belief through, it becomes 'true' and an audience, if it wishes, and if I am convincing, can also believe in that 'truth'.

I can take an ordinary object like a chair and decide to make-believe it is something else – a horse, or a motorbike, or a lawnmower – and act accordingly. I behave as if it 'really' were what I say it is. What is important is not the object itself but my *attitude* to it. That is what creates the 'reality' of the situation.

This is a natural, easy process. Children do it all the time. Adults will use simple objects on a tabletop to explain a football match – this pepper-pot is player number 9 etc. There is no problem, it is spontaneous.

My basic task as an actor, therefore, is to study the events the author has given in the script and to say, **What 'if'** . . . they were true?

Studying the play proceeds in three main phases, each of which has a specific creative goal.

Phase One
Creative Goal: 'I am being'†

The early, and in many ways most important, part of the process consists in an exploration of the action of the play as a whole.

Given Circumstances
I have to work with other actors to explore the script, to find out what happens, what the sequence of events is as the writer saw it. What are the life circumstances, the **Given Circumstances**, of the characters we are playing?

Before-time, After-time
We also have to supply what the writer has left out. We need to know what has happened before the scene opens – the **Before-time** – and what will happen after the play is over – the **After-time**. Each of us must then be able to summarise the action of the play, briefly and concisely.

Supertask
The company must then decide what the play is about. What is its subject, its theme?

What is its **Supertask**?

† This is a case of Stanislavski inventing or rather reviving a lost word. The verb to be now only exists in Russian in the infinitive, *est'*. Stanislavski uses the first person singular, *ja esm'*, which no one would normally use. 'I am being' is a way of conveying this usual usage.

Episodes and Facts

Once a sense of the play as a whole and its meaning have been established, more detailed work can begin. We need to see how the action unfolds, what its components are, so that we can work on it more easily. We first divide the action of the play into major **Episodes**, the main building blocks of the action. Then we divide the **Episodes** into **Facts**,† to show what happens at each moment in an **Episode**.

Basic Actions and Tasks

Once I and the other actors know what happens, what the situation demands, we have to define what it is the characters have to do in each **Episode**, their **Basic Action**; what they have to do in each **Fact**, their **Task**; and then the **Actions** they perform to fulfil their **Task**.

The sequence we have defined – the events which make up the play, the **Tasks**, the **Actions** the characters must perform to accomplish them – must then be made *personal, essential* to each of us. I must find ways of *making my* **Tasks** *essential to me*, of creating the **Necessity** for what I do.

Since there is no 'character' out there somewhere, only me on a stage in an imaginary situation, my initial exploration of the play must be as myself, as *me*. To turn fiction into fact for me, I must ask myself at every point in the play, 'If this situation were true, what would *I* do?' and I must always answer in the present, in what Stanislavski called the **Here, Today, Now**. The more precise my understanding of the situation, the more precise my response to it, my behaviour, will be.

I do this through discussion with the other actors and improvisation.

As a simple starting point I can use six questions:

Whence:	Where have I just come from?
Where:	Where am I?

---

† Stanislavski sometimes referred to both **Episodes** and **Facts** as '**Events**': *Episode (Event)*, *Fact / Event*.

What:	What am I doing?
Why:	Why am I doing it?
When:	When is this happening? What time of day, month, year? In which period?
Whither:	Where am I going to now?

Through-action

I then look at all my actions to see if they create a logical sequence, the **Through-action** that will ensure the coherence of the character.

Inner Monologue, Mental Images

Next I have to create the thoughts that lie behind my actions. What am I thinking at every point? What is my **Inner Monologue**? What pictures do I see in my head, what are my **Mental Images**?

All this I do, as myself, in the **Here, Today, Now**.

This process will produce a series of emotions and states of being by natural organic processes.

Emotion Memory

I can deepen my feelings and reactions by remembering experiences in my own life which are similar to those the character is going through, by using my **Emotion Memory**.

Subtext

My **Inner Monologue,** my **Mental Images** and **Emotion Memory** combine to produce the **Subtext**, everything that goes on in my mind during the action.

Through-Emotion

The sequence of emotions and feelings which I experience, running parallel to my sequence of actions, creates the **Through-emotion** which corresponds to the **Through-action**.

By following this process through methodically I become involved in the action. The situations take on a reality for me, I believe in them, my mind begins to accept them as true. There comes a point when the borderline between me and the 'character' is blurred. I am in the state Stanislavski called **'I am Being'**. At that point a kind of creative spontaneity occurs. The subconscious takes over. I behave with the same immediacy as I do in life but with the difference that my behaviour is selective, shaped, aesthetic and transparent.

'I am' is living. **'I am Being'** is acting.

Stanislavski felt that if Phase One was successfully completed, half the battle of creating a role was won. It should, therefore, take up 50 per cent of rehearsal time. In terms of Stanislavski's own practice, this meant a minimum of six months.

Phase Two
Creative Goal: The Third Being

Analysing the Script

In Phase One the dialogue and moves are all improvised. In Phase Two, the structure and style of the text must be examined, its distinctive features explored, and the author's words must be married to the actions, physical and mental, that have been planned.

External Characterisation

At the psychological core of the performance will always be me, but I will have to give physical form to my inner characterisation. My external behaviour and appearance may not be mine. Age, physique, looks will be defined by the script, including make-up and costume.

I will not always appear in contemporary plays. Manners, fashions, ways of thinking, beliefs change from period to period and I may need to study and to shape my external appearance and mannerisms accordingly. I will need to understand the codes of conduct in force when the play was written, the ideas and values that were current then but which may have disappeared since. I will need to know what books were read, what paintings there were, what music was heard, what houses looked like, what personal hygiene was like.

Staging

Moves are still improvised, changing from rehearsal to rehearsal, prompted by the characterisation and new discoveries about the interplay of the characters.

Tempo-rhythm

Each action, thought, feeling has its own specific pace, its **Tempo-rhythm**. This must be determined as its affects the character, the colour of what is done.

At this point the **Third Being**, the actor/role begins to emerge, the combination of my own life experience and imagination, physical characterisation and the written script.

Phase Three
Creative Goal: The Creative Actor in the Play

Planning and Perspective

Over the period of rehearsal the play has gradually been broken down, taken apart, examined, since the moment when the subject or **Supertask** was defined. It now has to be put together again and given artistic shape.

This is the phase of **Perspective** or **Planning**. The director, with the actors, now needs to consider the shape of the performance as a whole. The improvised moves used in Phase Two have to be replaced by fixed patterns in line with the director's concept and the environment created by the set, costume, sound and lighting designers. I and all the other actors need to be sure about our **Through-actions**. Have they been lost in the welter of small actions we have prepared? Do we still have a clear sense of direction? What should be in the foreground? What should be in the background? What are the high, the low points? What are the moments of intensity, of relaxation? Are the relative **Tempo-rhythms** right? Is the emotional curve of the play expressed in the staging?

During Phase Three the cast gradually strip away all unnecessary detail, all the clutter, until only what is essential and truly expressive remains, so that what happens on stage is clear and can be read by an audience.

Finally, the company have to verify whether the **Supertask** they provisionally defined is correct in the light of their deeper knowledge of the play. If it is not, they change it.

I now become a creative actor in the play.

This process can be expressed diagrammatically, as shown on the following page. It is also discussed in greater detail in Part Three.

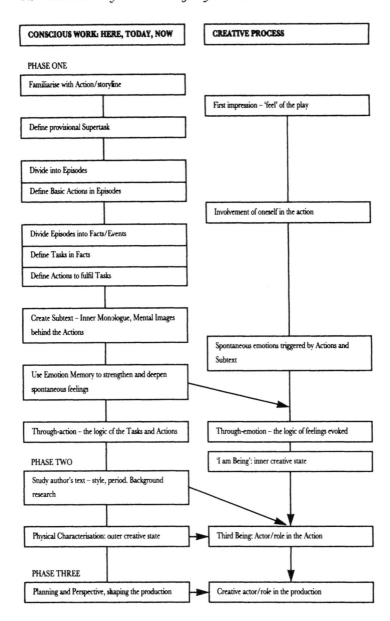

PART TWO
The Stanislavski 'system'

I cannot use the Method of Physical Action effectively unless I am in full control of my art, my technique. For that I must master the Stanislavski 'system' which provides the technical means by which to create and communicate the **Dramatic 'I'**. At the Studio, students spent almost two years studying it before they were allowed to begin to work on plays.

Stanislavski believed the ideal actor to be someone who is in control, who has mastered his craft and achieved total artistic independence. He also believed actors to be responsible for the maintenance and development of their skills. Students cannot just be passive recipients, dutifully obeying the tutors. *They* are the ones in class, *they* are doing the exercises and the improvisations. If they do not commit themselves fully to this work, if they are not actively engaged in it, they are wasting their own and everybody else's time. Actors cannot just be pawns or puppets manipulated by directors. They must use rehearsal work as a basis for their own private work, which they then feed back into the production.

There are two aspects to the technique of the 'system'; one inner, where the mind and imagination create the thoughts and feelings of the character; the other outer, where the body expresses and communicates what is going on inside. It is no good my carrying imaginative and subtle thoughts and feelings inside me if they are not reflected in the minutest detail in my body.

Actors need to be finely tuned instruments, responsive to every changing impulse, every leap of the imagination. A virtuoso pianist will not play on a piano which is out of tune or is missing strings, or which has two notes stuck together, so that when he plays the note C, B and possibly C♯ sound as well. He wants a first-rate concert grand. We have to become our own concert grands.

Stanislavski assumed that serious actors, like musicians, dancers and athletes, would continue to do exercises, physical and mental, throughout their career to keep their technique, their control over voice and body sharp, their instrument finely tuned.

As I begin training my own instrument, I must take nothing for granted, least of all myself, my own mind and body. For the musician, the instrument is out there, it is a physical object to be mastered. It makes demands: fingers have to control the key-board, the strings; feet the pedals; hands the bow. My problem is that I live in my instrument, I don't think about it, except when I am ill or it doesn't work properly. It is just there. But do I really know it? I have to learn to look at it from the outside for a while, to see what it is, what it does, what its creative possibilities are.

Stanislavski often referred to the openness, the naivety, of the child. The process of becoming an actor is, in a sense, the process of becoming a child again, doing everything as though for the first time. I need to be as open as a child exploring a new world but, at the same time, I have consciously to experience myself, to realise what is happening in my own mind and body, my organism, so I can use it as an artist. I must be a knowing child.

When teaching the 'system', Stanislavski divided it up into what he sometimes called 'Elements'. Acting is a complex combination of skills, too complex to be taken in all at once. The Elements have to be separated out, studied and mastered individually and then put back together again in a coherent technique.

The study of each element falls broadly into two phases:

1. Exercises to examine what people actually do in life; what the mechanism is and how it works.
2. Exercises to see how imaginative, artistic use can be made of that mechanism in various dramatic situations.

One result of these exercises is that I build up vocabularies, a resource base not only of words but also of actions, movements, memories, so that they are readily available and can quickly be referred to during rehearsal.

The study of the Elements of the 'system' must run, as at the Studio, in parallel with classes in voice movement, dance, acrobatics, fencing, play analysis and text study which provide physical, vocal and intellectual skills without which the 'system' is meaningless.

In Part Two the explanatory material at the beginning of each section is my own.

The exercises selected from Novitskaya's account of work at the Opera-Dramatic Studio, *Uroki Vdoxnovenija* (pp. 222–377), are indicated as 'Studio Exercises'. Practical examples of the way these exercises were done at the Studio are marked 'Studio Notes'.

Exercises which I have modified, in order to update them (see introduction) are marked with an asterisk. All other exercises are my own, based on Stanislavski's originals.

These exercises are not exhaustive, but they are models for others which any group can create. At the First Studio, which Stanislavski founded in 1912, and which nurtured a group of young actors and directors who were to become the leading teachers of acting for the next forty years, there was a large book, left permanently on display, in which the members could write down suggestions for exercises and improvisations. It was freely used. The vitality of the First Studio lay in its willingness to experiment. That is an example worth following.

Physical Action

Physical action is the basis of acting. This is what an audience sees, interprets – movement, stance, gesture – to understand the meaning of the play. The body language of the cast will convey much of that meaning, even if, for some reason, the dialogue cannot be heard, or understood.

The body needs to carry out our intentions and express the state of mind, the mood, in which we carry them out. Awareness and control are essential factors in our technique.

These classes study:

Release and relaxation
Using muscles
Combined action
Intention and justification
Actions

RELEASE AND RELAXATION

A precondition for any creative work is a free, flexible body. A blocked body cannot express anything except its own rigidity.

In our nightmares when we are in danger we are 'paralysed' with fear. We want to run away but we are 'rooted to the spot'. We want to shout for help but no sound comes out of our mouth. One of the actor's greatest difficulties is sheer terror, stage fright which never goes away, indeed for some it gets worse as their fame increases.

This is not an experience which is confined to actors. Watch a group of 'ordinary' people who are suddenly exposed to public attention. They have to walk across a bare space, some ten or twelve feet, to collect an award or a prize with a hall full of people watching them. They suddenly become self-conscious. Their walk is uncoordinated. What are they to do with their hands? Politicians are sometimes asked just to 'walk past camera' before they are interviewed. Their walk, nine times out of ten, is unnatural, their eyes glassy. They have been asked to walk and that is what they do, walk, but they suddenly become aware of the fact that they are walking and that the camera crew and later, thousands of viewers, are watching them. An everyday activity suddenly becomes an endurance test. The body tenses. It has become an alien, almost a hostile object. It no longer seems to belong to us.

How are we to get back control of our body? The answer is first learn how to release tension, free the muscles and relax at will. Then we can do what we want, we can feel in control and not the victim of some mysterious force which is taking our body and our voice away from us.

Relaxation is a technique that, over a period of time, can be learned and mastered. It is largely a matter of awareness. The object is to achieve relaxation and only to use, at will, those muscles which are absolutely necessary to carry out a particular action. It is the principle of minimum effort for maximum effect.

Stanislavski planned his work on relaxation and muscular control in several phases.

Phase One: Awareness of Tension

One of the problems with tension is that most of the time we are unaware of it. We see it in other people, but not always in ourselves. The first step is to become consciously aware of what tension is and feels like, and of the effect it has on our ability to function.

In doing these exercises, don't try to analyse what you are doing, just feel your body.

STUDIO EXERCISES
Experiencing total tension:
■ Stretch out on the floor, tense as hard as you can until it is painful, then release. Repeat, trying each time to experience the difference between tension and relaxation, and, in particular, the pleasure of release.

Necessary and unnecessary tension:
A level of tension is necessary in certain muscles for us to be able to do anything at all. But other muscles should be free. If I only want to clench my fist I don't need to tense my knees. Explore this:

■ Walk round the room, see where the unnecessary tensions are and try to release them.
■ Sit on the arm of a chair, see where the unnecessary tensions are and try to release them.

Extreme physical tension has an effect on our ability to think and operate mentally. Explore this:

■ Tense all your muscles and **a.** count backwards from 100, subtracting first 1, then 2, then 3, then 4, then 5 etc. **b.** perform mental calculations as other members of the group feed information to you, operation by operation e.g. $1 + 7 - 3 + 2 \times 12 + 5 + 9$ etc.
■ Take an object that someone hands you. As you tense your muscles to grasp it and take it towards you, multiply 17 by 120.

Phase Two: The Monitor

You cannot give a performance successfully if you are thinking about your muscles all the time, any more than you can function in life. But part of your mind has to be aware of what is happening to you, if you are tensing. The aim is to develop an internal monitor that, in time, will automatically detect and release tensions during rehearsal and performance without conscious effort.

The External Monitor

STUDIO EXERCISES
As a preliminary, perform a series of simple actions while someone else acts as your Monitor, pointing out unnecessary tensions to you as you go. Verify what they say. Is there tension where they say it is? Become aware of it and release it.

■ Pace out the size of the room taking normal steps.
■ Line up chairs against the wall.
■ Tidy up the room.
■ Open and shut a window, a door.

Perform this and similar exercises until you get to the point at which you can almost tell where the tensions are before you are told.

The Internal Monitor

The next step is to become completely self-reliant, to develop our own internal monitor and control our muscles at will, and learn to select, move and control the parts of the body independently. The aim of all these exercises is to become aware of what is happening to your own body.

STUDIO EXERCISES

■ Either sitting or walking round the room, in turn tense the neck, shoulder and back muscles, the right leg and left arm, then the left leg and right arm. Tense simultaneously the muscles of the right leg and left arm and vice versa. Transfer tension from the right to the left leg.

■ Sit upright and pull back your shoulders. Check which of your back muscles are working. Repeat several times. In the same position move first your right shoulder, then your left, the arms should do nothing.

■ 'Puppets'. This is an exercise in tensing the whole body. One student adopts a position and tenses his whole body like a puppet. Another student carries the 'puppet' to another part of the room. The 'puppet' must not budge, and the body must not relax.

■ 'Rag doll'. An exercise in total relaxation. The students are rag dolls, hanging from nails. They are taken from the nails and thrown to the floor.

■ Exercise with an imaginary fence. First crawl under the imaginary fence, which is, say, 40 cm above the ground, gradually pushing your head and shoulders under it. Then crawl back under the fence backwards.

■ The 'kitten'. Get down on all fours. First lazily roll on your

back and stretch, like a cat, and then contract. Then, arch
your back, hiss and adopt a defensive position.

■ Stand against the wall and on a count of 4, 8,16, 32, gradually
bend forward and on the same count, unbend. Do this
exercise again in a sitting position. First the head drops, then
the neck bends, the first vertebra, the second etc.

■ Check your hands:

    a. Extend each finger individually. Bend each finger in
       turn.

    b. Shake a drop of water off your hand. Fan your face with
       your hands as though it were hot; shoot a pistol.

    c. Interlock your fingers and make a continuous wavy
       movement.

■ With the rest of your body at rest, move one hand, one foot,
your head etc.

■ Trace letters with the big toe of your right foot on your left
foot (A, Q, B, W). Do the same with your left foot.*

Phase Three: Balance and the Centre of Gravity

Actors need a firm sense of balance and the ability to transfer
weight without losing control or equilibrium. Every sequence of
moves or actions requires a flow of energy (weight) from one
part of the body to another. The crucial factor in maintaining
balance is a knowledge of the centre of gravity.

Locating the Centre of Gravity

STUDIO EXERCISES
In each case, the exercises must be performed using only essential
muscular effort. There should be no unnecessary tensions
elsewhere.

■ Take two chairs and place them three feet apart. Place one
knee on one chair, stretch out and grasp the other chair and at
the same time lift the other leg off the ground. Perform a series
of movements while maintaining the centre of gravity.

■ Kneel on a chair, keep one hand on the chair. The other does not quite reach the floor, so bend down to pick up a piece of paper.

■ In a kneeling position, reach up towards a hanging object without letting your feet leave the floor.

■ Lean forward and hand a book to someone some distance away while sitting.

■ In a sitting position, reach out and take a book from the table.

■ In a sitting position stretch out as far as you can to pick up some flowers that are:
   • On the window-sill.
   • Lying on the floor in the corner.

■ Go up and down stairs, a step at a time, slowly, then quickly.

■ Get down on your knees in the middle of the room, then, on cue, start to get up and imagine that you receive a blow in the back or the chest. Do you fall or manage to stay upright? Where is your centre of gravity?

■ Imagine you are sitting down and someone tries to push you off your chair. The chair tilts but remains upright. Where is your centre of gravity?

You should experiment with these and similar exercises at home until you become expert at locating your centre of gravity.

Shifting the Centre of Gravity

As we change activity, as we progress from one action to another, the centre of gravity shifts.

STUDIO EXERCISES

Make sure the positions are spontaneous and not preplanned.

■ Lean on a chair and find where the points of balance are (elbows, feet).

■ Lean against the wall and find the points of balance (spine, feet).

■ Stand up straight on both legs, shift the centre of gravity to your left leg, then your right. Stand on one leg, prepare to run.

■ Everyone is sitting at rest. On cue, everyone takes a position as though rooted to the spot.

■ Everyone stands against the wall. One student grabs each of

the others in turn, drags them to the middle of the room and
sets them in a position as though they had just landed on the
floor. Where is the centre of gravity?
■ Run round the room and suddenly come to a halt at an
agreed spot (on the brink of a precipice).
[Make sure the positions are spontaneous and not preplanned.]

USING MUSCLES

Phase four: The Right Muscles for the Specific Activity

We now need to look more closely at the question of necessary
and unnecessary tensions and see which muscles should be
working in any given activity and those which should not. Use
the Internal Monitor.

STUDIO EXERCISES
■ Sit at a table. Put your hands on it. Pick up a box (or a pencil)
just as you would in life.
■ Pick up a vase, a clock, a book, glasses etc.
■ Brush crumbs, dust from your lap.
■ Throw a crumpled ball of paper on to the floor or somewhere
particular (into a drawer, a basket).
■ Retrieve a handkerchief from the water.
■ Go down on your hands and knees and grope for a hole.
■ Try to discover with your knee whether there are any puddles.
■ Cross a small bridge at night on which many planks are
missing.
■ Reach for a nail high up on the wall.
■ Recall your favourite sport and which muscles are used.
Reproduce the actions involved as accurately as possible.

Muscular Contractions when Working with Heavy Objects

Example:
- Carry a real chair from the wall to the table. Which muscles are involved? Then carry an imaginary chair, using the same muscular effort and the same level of energy. If you don't succeed, repeat the exercise with a real chair and try again.

The following exercises should be performed first with real, then imaginary objects.
- Carry a small table.
- Move a table over to the wall.
- Move a heavy picture, draw a blind, a curtain.
- Open a piano lid.
- Shift a cupboard on your own.
- Drag a heavy trunk.
- Pick up a box, a suitcase, a bucket of water.
- Hammer a stake into the ground.
- Knock a nail into the wall and remove it with pincers.
- Wring out wet washing.
- Dig the garden.
- Haul a heavy object out of the water.

It is essential to know the nature of the objects you are using, and what specific muscular effort is required, so that even if the object in not 'real', the muscular effort is accurate.

In performance, suitcases that are supposed to be heavy are often empty, and rocks that are lifted are made of light plastic. Placing the body in the right positions and contracting the appropriate muscles creates the illusion of the object.

COMBINED ACTION

Many of our actions on stage are performed with other people. We have to learn to adapt and coordinate our actions to theirs. Let us look at this, working first in pairs and then in groups. The actions are mimed but the muscular effort should be as precise as possible.

Coordination

Working in pairs:
- Saw wood, drag a large chest, a sofa, move a cupboard, row a boat, play tennis, play ball.
- Pass heavy objects to each other, changing objects all the time – a heavy trunk, bricks, a bucket of water. Decide what it is you have to do. When you change objects, change your intention (why am I doing this?).

Working as a group:
- Tidy up the garden: plant trees, shrubs, dig trenches, move material in wheelbarrows.
- On a building site: lay bricks, cement, erect wooden frames.

Physical Contact and Conflict

We need to be aware of how muscles operate when we come into contact, or conflict with another actor so that we can avoid doing actual damage, say, during a fight or a struggle.

Each exercise should first be performed with physical contact and the operation of the muscles studied. Repeat precisely without actual physical contact.
- A student adopts a defensive position, feet firmly planted on the ground. Another student tries to shoulder him out of the way. Each must state which muscles were in operation. Repeat the exercise without actual physical contact. The muscles must operate in precise sequence.
- Try very hard to knock your partner over. Try not so hard.
- Pull your partner off his chair.
- Grab your partner and draw him to you.
- Stop and avoid someone coming at you.
- Join hands and force your partner down on his knees.
- Remove your hand from your partner's hand. Grab a chair a book, a letter.

- Free your legs from your partner's grasp.
- Clasp your hands behind your back.
- Free your hand from a rope.
- Suddenly rush out of a corner at your partner from behind. Free yourself from him as he suddenly falls.
- Play tug of war.

In certain plays there is a physical struggle between actors. For example, in *A Midsummer Night's Dream*, Hermia has to be restrained from attacking Helena when the four lovers quarrel. This is a difficult scene either because people can actually be hurt if it spins out of control, or because it can be so tame that the energy and violence of the scene are lost. The scene can only be played effectively if the actors know which muscles to use and how to control them, so that they look violent without actually being so.

INTENTION AND JUSTIFICATION

Every physical action performed on stage, every positioning of the body proceeds as follows:

1. There is excess tension produced by the fact of being on stage.
2. That tension is automatically released by the Internal Monitor.
3. The action or position is justified by the creation of an intention.

We have looked at 1 and 2. Now we need to examine 3.

STUDIO EXERCISES
- Students sit in a row. On a given signal they take up a position. On a second signal they investigate how the body is balanced, see how much tension is necessary to maintain their position and remove any excess tension. They then give meaning to their actions by responding to questions.

Question: How do you justify your position? What is your action? Your eyes are fixed on the floor. What are you afraid of? Why are your hands outstretched as though you were going to defend yourself, when you are sitting down?

Answer: I am sitting on the seashore. My friends have left me to enjoy the sun. My legs are paralysed. Suddenly I see a crab crawling towards me . . .

STUDIO EXERCISES

Divide the group into halves: 'directors' and 'actors'.

■ The directors place the actors in specific positions which the actors then have to justify.

■ Reverse roles.

The positions originally adopted merely as positions have become *action* because they have been justified, they have an intention.

ACTIONS

We now need to examine the nature of our actions, starting with our everyday behaviour. Most of the actions we perform, some 90 per cent, are automatic, reflex (Part One). Many of them are **Organic Actions**. We must first, therefore, become conscious of what we have been doing unconsciously and examine our behaviour.

EXPLORATORY EXERCISE

■ Take a short period of time in your daily life (for example, preparing to come to class, from the time you get up to the moment you leave the house). Write down the sequence of actions you perform. Could they be performed in any other order? For example, you might have breakfast before you shower or vice versa, but are there sets of actions that cannot be performed in any other order?

Becoming Aware of Organic Actions

Let us now look more consciously at individual **Organic Actions**. One of the most effective means of doing this is to mime any objects we use. The absence of the object makes us think about it, and not take it for granted.

Exploratory Exercise
■ Take an actual item of clothing, e.g. a coat. Put it on, noting carefully everything you do. When you think you know what the sequence of actions is, put the coat aside and mime the action as accurately as possible. If you don't succeed, go back to using the real item, becoming aware of the logical chain of actions. Repeat until you get it right.

Studio Exercises
■ Take a series of simple, everyday **Organic Actions** and break them down into their smallest constituent actions:
  • Write a letter.
  • Peel potatoes.*
  • Wash the dishes.*
  • Shave/put on your make-up.*
  • Pack a suitcase.
  • Play a musical instrument.

In these exercises it is essential not to skip any action, however trivial. It is not a question of how fast you do them but how thoroughly, how knowingly, you do them.

Psychologically Simple and Psychologically Complex Actions

So far we have only looked at the mechanics of these actions; we studied *what* we do, as a kind of laboratory experiment. In the theatre, as in life, *how* we perform actions is determined by time, place and circumstance, which alter the speed, mood, the emotional tone of what we do.

We can perform actions for psychologically simple or complex reasons. For example, cleaning up a room involves **Organic Actions**.

The reason for performing these actions can be simple or complex:

We can clean up:
- Our own room to please our mother who has been away – a simple psychological task.
- The room of a close friend who has died unexpectedly – a complex psychological task.

STUDIO EXERCISES
Establish the sequence of **Organic Actions** – *what* you do – and see how changed circumstances influence *how* you do them.

■ Preparing a meal:

- Prepare an ordinary meal.
- Prepare a favourite meal for someone you love.
- Prepare a special meal for a sick relative.

■ Burning papers:

- Burn old, unwanted papers in the fireplace.
- Burn books, newspapers, old note-books etc. to warm the room.
- Burn incriminating documents before anyone finds them.*

■ Reading the newspaper:

- To see if there is anything about a famous person you admire.
- To find a review of a play you have just seen [you will need to make up the review in your head].
- To see if there is any news of a relative/friend who may have been involved in an air/car crash [you will need to make up the article].

■ Pack a suitcase, repeating exactly the same actions as in the earlier exercise (p. 27).
Where are you going? For how long? What is the climate? What kind of clothes do you need? Is this a holiday? Business? Do you really want to go or not?

■ Take off your overcoat.
- You have come home from work and are hungry.

- You have just come from visiting a very sick friend in hospital.
- You are in the waiting-room of a famous producer and you want him to give you a job.*
- It is a new, rather expensive coat and you want to take good care of it.

The Logic of Dramatic Action

We now need to take these exercises a stage further by bringing them together in a simple dramatic situation.

STUDIO EXERCISES
You are expecting your girlfriend's/boyfriend's parents for a meal for the first time. You want to make a good impression. *
The sequence of **Basic Actions**:
  1. Tidy the room.
  2. Lay the table.
  3. Make yourself presentable.
  4. Check to see if everything is all right.
  5. Wait for them to arrive.
Each of these five **Basic Actions** can be broken down into sequences of small, physical actions:
1. Tidy the room:
   - Look round the room and decide where to begin.
   - Tidy away all the objects left lying about.
   - Vacuum the floor.
   - Dust the furniture.
Even here you can break down the action further. For example, where is the vacuum cleaner kept? What kind is it? You have to assemble it and take it apart after use and put it away again. Where are the dusters kept etc?
2. Lay the table:
   - Wash your hands after cleaning up.
   - Put a clean cloth on the table.
   - Put flowers, a decoration, candles on the table.
   - Set knives, forks and spoons, plates, glasses, napkins. (Where are they kept?)

- Open a bottle of wine.
3. Make yourself presentable:
    - Go to the bathroom.
    - Look at yourself in the mirror. Do you need a shave? Is your make-up all right? Should you clean your teeth?
    - Go to the bedroom.
    - Select something suitable to wear. (What will make the best impression?)
    - Comb and tidy your hair.
4. Check to see if everything is all right:
    - Go to the dining-room.
    - Double-check the table, alter it if you need.
    - Make sure the chairs are all in line.
    - Light the candles.
5. Wait:
    - Sit and read a book, newspaper. (Where do you get them?)
    - Look at the clock.
    - Listen for the doorbell or the telephone to ring.

Run through this sequence in your mind several times until it is clear, then act it out.

A series of exercises can be created on this model. The situations should be based on everyday experience and not stray too far from the familiar, as that introduces problems too complex to handle at this stage.

STUDIO EXERCISES
In the following exercises:
    1. Define what you want.
    2. Define the **Basic Action(s)** that will give you what you want.
    3. Perform the actions necessary to fulfil it.

■ You are lost in an unfamiliar part of the town in which you live. You need to get home.

■ You are going to a very special party. Your favourite suit/dress is locked in the wardrobe. Where is the key? You are alone in the house.

■ Thieves have broken in and left you tied up. You need to get free and call the police.

■ You are playing with your dog in the garden and trample down your sister's favourite flowers. She must not find out you were responsible.

■ Your flat is being decorated. You forget and lean against a freshly painted door. Get rid of the paint.

■ You have gone to visit a friend. He or she isn't in. You have more than an hour to wait. Occupy your time.

Mental Action

These classes study:
Focus and concentration
Imagination
The subtext
Emotion Memory

FOCUS AND CONCENTRATION

Our world is the acting space. That is where our concentration should be, not backstage, not in the audience but there in the make-believe world we have created. Our concentration on the people and objects in the acting space focuses the audience's attention, directing it where it should go so that the play makes sense.

Just like muscular relaxation and control, the ability to focus and to control and direct concentration is one of the most fundamental skills an actor must acquire.

Sportsmen, footballers, tennis players know that however many people are watching, however much noise and shouting there is, their sole task is to make sure the ball goes where they want it to.

Actors must similarly be able to focus totally on what they are doing at any given moment, on the 'now'. They also need to be able to switch focus rapidly to the next 'now' moment. The performance is a succession of 'now' moments.

Focus, concentration must be continuous from curtain up to curtain down. The sharper it is, the sharper the audience's focus and experience of the play will be.

Focus can be studied in four phases:

1. Focusing in the real world.
2. Focusing in the imaginary world.
3. Multi-level focus.

4. Focusing as a means of developing new aspects of a role.

Any person or thing on which we focus is called the **Object of Attention**.

Focusing in the Real World

STUDIO EXERCISES
■ You are given an object and asked to study it. You then have to describe its shape, colour, use, special features. The object is then removed and you are asked to tell the group what you remember, what caught your attention. You are then given the object again and a comparison is made between the real object and the remembered object.
■ Study people in a picture postcard or a newspaper photograph. The picture is taken away. Describe what you saw. Compare your description with the picture.

Focus with Each of the Five Senses

STUDIO EXERCISES
Visual focus:
■ Observe the other students in the group. Study the person next to you attentively – what he is wearing, what colour his clothes are, how he is sitting.
■ Observe an object in the room e.g. the carpet, the wallpaper, the curtains. Close your eyes and describe the pattern from memory.
■ Observe the figures in a picture and do as they do. [If there is a large group in the picture, the students decide among themselves who is going to represent whom.]
■ Make a human figure out of matches and show it to the other students. Cover it. They must try and repeat what you have created. Uncover the original and compare their efforts with it.
■ 'Mirror'. Two students stand opposite one another. One performs a series of movements. The other acts as his 'mirror',

reflecting back what he does i.e. if Number 1 moves his right hand, Number 2 moves his left.
- ■ 'Shadow'. One student moves around the room, stops to say hello to someone, shakes his hand, waves goodbye etc. Another student follows, imitating all his movements.
- ■ One student adopts three poses, and inwardly justifies them. Another student observes, mentally repeats the movements in the same order and then finds his own justification for them. Compare the two justifications. Reverse the exercise.

Aural focus:
- ■ Listen to the sounds you hear from the street, from the corridor outside, remember them and report what you have heard.
- ■ Switch focus on a given signal, listening first to the street, then the corridor, then the room you are in, then the street again etc.
- ■ Use the sounds you have heard, ignoring anything you have seen, to reconstruct what you think is going on in the street, in the corridor or in the room.

Tactile focus:
Close your eyes.
- ■ Feel the back of the chair. Tell the group what its shape is, if there is any carving or moulding.
- ■ Feel the surface of the table to see if there is any damage, or scratches.
- ■ Take various coins and describe their shape and value.
- ■ Describe the letters which someone has scratched on to a piece of paper.
- ■ Try to separate out a single strand of hair from a lock.
- ■ Try to feel a needle on the table top.
- ■ Try to feel what the object is under the tablecloth.
- ■ Use your foot to locate a key under the carpet.
- ■ Use your foot to locate scratches on the polished floor.
- ■ 'The telephone'. Stand five students in a row and write one letter with your fingertip on the back of each to form a word e.g. TABLE. Check to see if the five can form the word.

Olfactory focus:

Close your eyes.

■ Take objects of various kinds – flowers, sweets, cosmetics, preserves – and state what they are by their smell only.

■ Are there any other smells in the room – damp, floor-polish, stale cigarette smoke?

Gustatory focus:

■ Taste various kinds of food, fruit and vegetables e.g. apples, potatoes, butter, bread, and state what they are. Can you tell the difference between two kinds of apple?

Group Focus

Sometimes a group of people have to focus on a shared activity, or a common object.

STUDIO EXERCISES

■ On a given signal, stand. On a second signal, pick up your chair. On a third, move round in a circle, keeping equal distance between you. The tutor will beat time and, from time to time, slow or increase the speed at which you move. On the command, 'Stop', you come to a halt until you are told to move again.

■ The tutor says, 'Form two lines opposite each other,' and beats time. It is important for you not to touch each other or jog each other with your chairs as you form up the two lines. On a signal, each of you stands in front of your chair. On another signal, you all move your chairs to the right and sit on them. This must be done without any noise or fuss.

■ On a signal, get up from your chair. On a second, pick up your chair. On a third, change places with the person opposite you.

■ On a signal, pick up your chair. On another, start to move with it and keep changing direction. Be careful that neither you nor the chair makes contact with anyone. On the third signal, carry your chair back to its original position and put it down.

Word Games

The object of these exercises is for members of the group to focus on each other so that they can act as one.

■ Distribute all the letters of the alphabet among the class – each student may have more than one letter. The tutor then selects a well-known quotation which the students have to spell out letter by letter, each using the letter(s) they have been given. For example:

If music be the food of love, play on,
Give me excess of it . . .*

Establish a tempo. The first student says, 'I', clapping at the same time. The second student says the letter 'F', clapping at the same time etc. Mark the spaces between words by the whole group stamping their feet. Once the quotation is complete, the group stand up. The group must carry the whole quotation in their head, and maintain the rhythm that was initially established. The whole should sound as though one person were speaking

Select more complex quotations.

Number Games

As with word games, the object of these exercises is for members of the group to focus on each other so that they can act as one.

Studio Exercises

■ Divide the class into groups of not more than nine people. Give each student a number from 1 to 9. Single numbers are indicated by clapping the hands, tens by stamping the foot, hundreds by raising a hand, e.g. when the tutor says, '2', the person to whom that number has been designated claps. For 27, Number 2 stamps his foot and Number 7 claps his hands. For 127, Number 1 raises his hand, Number 2 stamps his foot and Number 7 claps his hands.

■ Fifteen people sit in a semicircle. Ten are given the numbers 0 to 9, the other five are ascribed mathematical signs: +, −, ÷, ×, =. The group then perform mathematical operations e.g. the tutor says, '14 + 6'. First the Numbers for 10 (1 + 0) stand up, then Number 4 stands up, then the Sign for equals stands up, then the Numbers for 20 (2 + 0) stand up.

A regular rhythm should be maintained throughout all these exercises. You can increase the difficulty of the operations within the limits of the group's mathematical ability. The tempo can also be increased.

Focus – Observation – Retention

The object is to develop the ability to observe precisely, remember and reproduce.

Studio Exercises

■ Section off part of the room. Arrange the furniture and contents etc. Select two or three students and ask them to study the arrangement, then send them out of the room. While they are gone, the others rearrange everything. The absent students are recalled and asked to put everything back as it was. Check their results.

■ Arrange a number of objects on the table – books, pencils, pens, papers, mirrors, make-up. Five or six students go to the table and study the arrangement. Then, while they have their backs turned, or are out of the room, rearrange everything. On their return, they must put everything back as it was.

■ Divide the class into three groups:

Group 1 are the **Objects of Attention**.

Group 2 are the control group.

Group 3 are the observers.

Group 1 sit in a semicircle in the middle of the room.

Group 2 stand in front of them, one to one.

Group 3 observe.

Group 1 are given objects (newspapers, handkerchiefs, flowers, letters, hats) by Group 2 and asked to examine them in the most comfortable position. On a given signal they 'freeze'. Group 3 are then asked to observe the 'frozen' position and the way the objects are being held, then they leave the room.

Group 2, the control group, then alter the positions of the members of Group 1 and the way they are holding the objects. Group 3 returns, restores Group 1 to their original positions. Group 2 verifies the accuracy of what they do.

■ Form groups of four arranged in squares as follows:

2 4
1 3

Number 1 makes a clear movement e.g. raises a hand. He then makes a second movement e.g. bows, while Number 2 copies the first movement (raises a hand).

Number 1 makes a third movement e.g. throws a javelin, while Number 2 copies the second movement (bows) and Number 3 copies the first movement (raises a hand). Number 3 then bows and Number 4 raises a hand (copying Number 1's first movement), thus continuing the cycle i.e. Number 4 becomes Number 1 – then 2 becomes 3, 3 becomes 4 until you decide to stop.

Change the numbers within the groups so that each person has a chance to initiate the exercise.

Multi-level Focus

In life we appear to function on many levels at once. We can iron a blouse (level one), listen to the radio (level two), look at the thermometer on the wall to see what temperature the room is (level three) etc.

Similarly, in the theatre we can have multi-level or split focus. For example, at the opening of *Three Sisters*, Olga is marking school books, remembering the previous year, looking out of the window at the weather and talking to her sister Irina.

STUDIO EXERCISES
■ Take a box of matches, count how many there are and tell a story at the same time.
■ Each student is given a sheet of paper with a mathematical problem on it (e.g. 182 x 24) and required to solve it while

another student asks him questions which require precise, logical answers.

■ Each student is given a card with a number on it. Then each is allocated a specific task – doing a crossword puzzle, recalling and writing down a poem they know etc. Meanwhile, two students engage in a conversation. The tutor calls out a number. The student with that number has to stand up and repeat the last thing that was said in the conversation.

■ Each student but one is given a length of string and asked to tie a number of complicated knots in it. The one singled out watches how the knots are tied and at the same time describes a painting. As this student is talking the tutor gives him a piece of string and asks him to tie the knots just seen.

■ Create a barrier out of tables, chairs and objects. Four students are sent to one side and each asked to sing their favourite song. The rest of the group choose a leader and then play follow-my-leader through the barrier, imitating everything he/she does. Once through the barrier, the group must say who sang what.

■ Each student is given a number. Take a poem everyone knows. The students recite it mentally. After two or three seconds the tutor calls a number. The student with that number stands up and starts to recite aloud until another number is called and that student takes over. The first student must, like all the others, continue to recite mentally. Further numbers are called. Each student should be called several times.

Circles of Attention

Our field of vision or hearing varies. We can focus on something very close, or on something far away, on a postage stamp or an open field. The spaces on which we concentrate are called **Circles of Attention**. They can be small, medium, large or very large.

We may need to focus down on a tabletop (small circle) or on the whole stage and auditorium (very large circle), according to the dramatic situation. We can be at the centre of the circle or outside it, at varying distances.

We need to be able to control the **Circle of Attention**, moving from the small to the very large, from looking at a jacket button to searching the horizon for someone we expect within a matter of seconds, without loss of focus.

STUDIO EXERCISES

When the circle is outside us:

- Place a number of objects on a table. Each member of the group is assigned one object to observe. All then turn their backs to the table and describe the object (**Object of Attention**).
- Ask the members of the group to observe all the objects on the table, then to describe them and their particular features (the small **Circle of Attention**).
- The members of the group observe the part of the room in which the table is placed and describe what they see (the medium **Circle of Attention**).
- The members of the group observe the entire room and describe what they see (large **Circle of Attention**).

When we are at the centre of the circle:

- Ask two members of the group to sit and observe each other and compare their clothing – small **Circle of Attention**.
- Bring in six or eight more people and ask them to observe everyone, including themselves. Establish the dominant colour in everyone's clothing – medium **Circle of Attention**.
- Involve the entire group and ask them to observe the way each, including themselves, is sitting – large **Circle of Attention**.

Reduce the time allotted to an exercise each time. Start with a count of 1 to 30 and reduce it to 1 to 5, to sharpen concentration.

Justifying Concentration

Just as there is no action without a reason, so there is no concentration without a reason. Concentration is for a purpose, it is action. You cannot concentrate in a void, your eyes glaze over after a while, you cannot focus. To concentrate for any length of time you must have a reason. You must create a situation in which you feel compelled to concentrate and finally to take some kind of action e.g. use the object.

STUDIO EXERCISES
There are three phases in these exercises:
1. Selecting the object.
2. Creating the imaginary situation.
3. Taking action.
■ Select one object from a number on the table and create a situation around it.
   • Object: A scarf.
   • Situation: You are going to the theatre tonight. You have a good dress and shoes. The scarf goes well with the dress, the colours match. These scarves are very fashionable. It looks good. You want to try it on to see if it goes with your complexion.
   • Action: Try it on.
■ • Object: A reproduction of a well-known painting, or a newspaper photograph.
   • Situation: Study the people in it, the way they are behaving, sitting, standing. Create the situation that led to this point.
   • Action: Act out the situation.

Contracting and Expanding the Circle of Attention: Justifying the Process

In any **Basic Action** we may need to focus differently as we perform individual actions, either by contracting or expanding the circle.

Contracting

STUDIO NOTES
Situation: There is a draught in the room. One of the window-panes is broken. Your task is to repair it.

*Action: First examine the wall in which there are three windows and locate the one that needs repairing (large **Circle of Attention**). Then focus on the middle window (medium **Circle of Attention**). Focus down on to the window-pane which keeps coming open in the wind (small **Circle of Attention**) then on the latch which is broken (**Object of Attention**). Set to work.*

Expanding

STUDIO NOTES
Situation: you want to give your twelve-year-old niece a present. She loves books. You know that she especially likes travel books. You have a good collection.
Action: You are sitting at your desk. You can see the book Life in the Arctic. *Has she read it (**Object of Attention**)? You recall that she has already borrowed it. You look at the other books on your desk (small **Circle of Attention**) but there is nothing suitable. Then you turn and look at the books on your bedside table and on the chair next to the desk (medium **Circle of Attention**). Nothing but newspapers. Then you look at the bookcase at the left end of the wall, at the dresser, on the floor . . . (large **Circle of Attention**).*

Circles of Attention in Performance

In performance we need to know what the **Object of Attention** is at any point, how wide the **Circle of Attention** is, and, as in the studio exercises, switch focus accordingly.

An ability to control the focus also helps us maintain full concentration. Any actor knows that there are occasions when concentration slips, and the performance becomes fuzzy. At that point, reduce the **Circle of Attention** to the minimum and focus on a small **Object of Attention** within that circle until concentration is fully restored; then you can expand the **Circle of Attention** again.

Observation of Life as a Source of Creative Material

Observation and focus are closely linked. Wherever you are,

whatever you are doing, you should continually focus on anything that catches your interest and observe it closely. You need to stock up impressions and facts and store them away so you can use them later in working on a play. It is like learning vocabulary when you study a language.

How observant are you? Check and see.

Studio Exercises
■ Shut your eyes and say what your best friend, or the person sitting next to you, was wearing yesterday, the same day last week.
■ What changes have taken place in the street where you live recently?
■ Have you been back to a part of town you once knew well? What changes have taken place?
■ Think of two or three interesting people you have seen in the street, the train etc. What special characteristics, mannerisms, clothing, make-up interested you in each case? Describe them to the group.

Make it a practice to observe two or three things or people each day. Keep a notebook if you can.

IMAGINATION

The world of the theatre is an imaginary world. It is as rich, diverse and exciting as our imagination can make it. We are not all equal in our capacity to imagine. For some it is easy, for others more difficult. But whatever our natural starting point, we can develop our imaginative skills, like any other skills.

Using the Real World

We can exercise our imagination by setting it to work on our immediate surroundings and so produce new situations and new scenarios.

Studio Notes
We are in acting class. There are five factors in the situation: the tutor, the

students, the room, the time of day, the season. We can change each factor in turn e.g.

1. Change the room. Suppose the class were being held in the theatre and not in the school.

The scenario: The company are away on their usual summer tour and its place has been taken by an out-of-town theatre. They are presenting Chekhov's The Cherry Orchard. *The students have been asked to play walk-ons in Act Three (the ball). They will work with their tutor on creating characters. Each students has to create a character, describe it to the tutor and the rest of the group, sketch the costume they would like. They have to create a logical sequence of actions to fit in with the production.*

2. Change the time of day.

The scenario: The rehearsal is taking place in the evening, not the morning. Tomorrow the students have to present some short scenes as part of their end-of-year assessment. They decide to work late until they are satisfied with the results. What arrangements will they make? How will they get home? What about their families? How will they let them know?†

3. Change the season. It is winter, not summer.

4. Change all the factors. Transform the situation into something else, using the physical environment:

  a. The academic year is over. We have decided to go to the forest and camp out overnight before saying goodbye for the summer.

  b. We take bedding, clothing, tents and food in our rucksacks.

  c. We all meet up at [?] station and take the [time?] train to [?].

  d. We make our way to a spot in the forest where there is a clearing and a stream and set up camp.

Transforming the room: The objects in the room must now be transformed in imagination into objects that fit the scenario. For example, the chairs become trees, the ceiling light becomes the moon/sun.

But what about the rest – the tables, windows, books, papers, scripts, pens, pencils, bags, briefcases, curtains?

† *Note*: If you decide to try this exercise, remember, all the details of the situation must be precise. It is not enough to answer the question, 'How will you get home?' with 'By bus' or 'By taxi'. Which bus? What time is the last bus? Where is the bus-stop? Where is the nearest taxi-rank? Do you have a telephone number to call one? Can you afford a taxi? Can you share with one or two other people? Can you walk?

Once the environment has been defined, each student must construct a series of logical, coherent actions in response to the question, 'What would I do if I were here in this forest?'. The response will require interaction with the other members of the group.

Once the exercise has been completed it should be reviewed to see if there was any vagueness or inconsistency. Any faulty passages should be reworked.

Object Exercises

STUDIO EXERCISES
With a single object:
■ Choose an object and build a scenario round it. The object must be sufficiently important to produce a complex story e.g. a valuable ring. Every action must be justified and where an action is not clear, questions must be asked until it is made clear.

STUDIO NOTES
Scenario: A student came down to the river with a bowl of washing. She put the bowl down on the little wooden platform at the river's edge, took off her shoes, and tucked up her skirt. She knelt down, having first cleaned the boards, and began to wash the linen.
Suddenly she stops and starts rummaging among the linen.
Question: Why has she started rummaging?
Answer: She has noticed that a ring is missing from her right hand. She mentally retraces her steps. Did she leave the ring at home? She didn't take it off and she remembers seeing it on her way to the river. Did she lose it when she tipped the washing out of the bowl on to the platform? She looks carefully through the washing again. Nothing. She thinks, then looks on and around the platform. Nothing. She thinks again then gets into the water and inspects the river-bed with her face close to the surface. She sees nothing. She examines her skirt, then stands still for a while.
Question: Why is she standing still?
Answer: Her movement has muddied the water and she is waiting for it to settle. She walks slowly, treading very carefully. She suddenly screws up her eyes and dives into the water.
Question: Why has she dived into the water?

Answer: She has spotted something shiny. She emerges from the water with sand cupped in her hands. She examines the sand but finds nothing. She dives in again and this time emerges with the ring in a pile of sand. She is delighted. She climbs back on to the platform, wrings out her sopping skirt, gathers up the washing, puts on her shoes and goes home.

STUDIO EXERCISES

Combining two activities:

■ Read a newspaper and listen to someone's conversation.

■ Think about something while trying to get warm.

■ Talk to someone while doing the washing-up.*

Combining an activity and an object. Incorporate the object into what you are doing:

■ Start to work on something – the telephone.

■ You are waiting for someone/something – a doll.

■ Get dressed – a light bulb.

Multiple objects:

■ Take two or three different objects and link them together to form a scenario. Select, for example, a mirror, a watch, a shirt, a bouquet of flowers, a handkerchief, a lottery ticket, an umbrella, keys, money . . .

STUDIO NOTES

A student is asked to build a scenario around a scarf, some cigarettes and some money.

Response:

The situation: I live with my sister. I have recently started my first job. I have just received my pay and I go out and buy a scarf as a present for my sister and some good cigarettes.

Action: I get home. I light a cigarette, empty out my spare change from my pocket. I keep five roubles back for myself and put the rest in the middle of the table where it can easily be seen. Then I unwrap the headscarf I am giving my sister. I take the lighted cigarette out of my mouth and carefully put it on the edge of the ashtray on the table. I pick up the scarf and admire it. I put it round my shoulders and go to the mirror to see what it looks like. I hear the doorbell. I throw the scarf on to the table and go to open the door. But it isn't my sister. I come back into the room. I can smell something burning. What is it? I rush to the table and grab the scarf. It has been lying on the burning cigarette and has a great hole in it. I do some quick thinking. I look at the clock. I put the money that was on the table in my pocket and the scarf in a drawer and dash to the shop to buy another scarf with the five roubles I had kept for myself.

Analysis: Analysing his own exercise, the student commented that whereas in theory action is supposed to give rise to thought and thought in turn to give rise to another action, he acted and thought simultaneously. For example, when he went to open the door he was thinking, 'It's her. I'll give her her present. She'll be very happy . . .' And he realised what was burning as soon as he smelt the smoke.

Using an Imaginary World

All the preceding exercises were based on familiar objects, activities and surroundings. However, work in the theatre often requires us to expand and develop the smallest indications. Sometimes all we are given in a script is: a street, a wood.

This is a disciplined process. What we imagine must be credible and logical.

STUDIO NOTES
Setting: A wood.
Three students were asked the following question: 'If you were out in the woods, what would you do?'
Answer 1: I am walking through the woods, pushing aside the branches as I go. I look for a clearing where I can sit down and rest. I try to find a comfortable spot in the shade. I see a little stream and go to it. I put down the bundle I am carrying. There is food in it. I roll up my sleeves, wet my hands and splash cool water on my face, then drink. I stretch out on the ground, clearing away the leaves and pine cones. I untie the bundle and start to eat. I watch the little birds and whistle at them in response to their song. Suddenly I am stung. I rub the spot but don't pay much attention to it. I turn on my side to sleep. I am stung again. I get up and find I have been sitting on an ants' nest. I decide to move somewhere else. I leave the clearing.
Answer 2: I am in the woods looking for mushrooms. I peer under the lower branches of a spruce, remove the moss and find the mushrooms I am looking

*for. I carefully cut them off with a knife and put them in a basket. When I
have collected quite a few I sit down on the grass beneath the tree and start to
clean the mushrooms with my knife. I put the mushrooms back into the basket,
cut a few young branches, cover the mushrooms with them and then go home.
Answer 3: I am going through the woods, singing and gathering flowers. I
stop, remove the scarf which is around my shoulders and put it on my head to
protect me from the sun. I sit on the ground and start to weave a garland with
the flowers. Suddenly I jump up and run off, scattering the flowers and
throwing away the unfinished garland.*

*Answers 1 and 2 are coherent and logical, although Answer 1 is more detailed
and shows a more active imagination. The end of Answer 3 comes out of
nothing. Why did she suddenly run off? What had happened?*

*The end has to be reworked so as to create a sequence of logically coherent
actions.*

*Answer 3 revised ending: I am sitting weaving a garland from the flowers I
have gathered. Suddenly it grows dark. I look up at the sky and see that storm
clouds have gathered and hidden the sun. What should I do? Run home or
wait for the storm to pass in the woods? Looking about me, I realise that the
trees are very young and won't protect me from the rain. The storm clouds
grow blacker and blacker and are coming near. I decide to make for home. I
have hardly gone a few steps when I feel that I have been hit on the back and
on the head. There are huge, scattered spots of rain. It starts to rain heavily.
What shall I do? Carry on? Soon I will be soaked to the skin. Again I look
for shelter and see a large spruce. I run towards it, scattering the flowers as I
go. The rain is heavy but doesn't last long. The sun soon comes out again. I
come out from under the spruce. Everything is soaking. I take off my shoes and
go home.*

The response is now logical.

We may only be given a situation in the very broadest terms e.g.
we are going on a journey.

   Not only do we have to imagine what the journey will be like,
we also have to feed our imagination with the information it
needs to work successfully.

EXERCISE
■ You are organising a long journey to a distant country e.g.
South America, Australia, or central Africa. You have to

consult books, maps, films, photographs, train timetables, shipping and airline schedules, to apply for visas and obtain currency. You will need to know something of the geography, politics and economics of the country you are going to. You will have to deal with practical problems like what to pack and what not to pack. This will mean consulting books, maps, looking at photographs and films.

Quick Responses

These exercises allow time for thought. Actors also need to develop the capacity for swift, spontaneous responses to suggestions and situations.

STUDIO EXERCISES

■ Hand students ordinary, everyday objects and suggest what they might be:
- A handkerchief – 'It's a mouse.'
- A small box – 'It's a frog.'
- A package – 'It's full of worms.'
- A glass of water – 'It's poison.'

■ Point to a student's head and say, 'There's a spider!'

The Before-time

One of the most important functions of the imagination is to supply what the writer has left out, the **Before-time**.

Initially we can experiment with dramatic situations of our own invention.

STUDIO NOTES
The dramatic situation: The audition.
You are at home alone one evening. Your parents have gone to the theatre. You want to enroll in a drama school but your parents are against it. You are preparing your entrance audition in secret. You only have two weeks left and you have to rehearse your speeches out loud. You have three hours. What are you going to do?
*You cannot play the situation fully unless you know the **Before-time**.*

The **Before-time**.

You came home. Your parents were wondering whether to go to the theatre or not. Your neighbours' daughter arrived with tickets for them. This is your chance. You tell your parents what an interesting play it is and that they shouldn't miss it. You explain to your neighbours' daughter that you have a lot of homework to do and don't have time to spend with her. You do all this with great 'sincerity'. You help your parents get ready and see them off.
Now you can play the audition.

STUDIO EXERCISES
- Take a well-known painting in which two or more people are involved in an activity (e.g. Cézanne's *The Card Players*) and create the **Before-time**.
- Take simple objects and describe where they came from, who might have used them.

STUDIO NOTES

*One member of the class has an old book. Where did it come from? What was the **Before-time** to his having it in class today?*
*The **Before-time**. A father bought it for his son from a well-known bookseller. His stamp is on the inside back cover. It is a travel book with good illustrations and was published in the nineteenth century. The bookseller acquired it after the original owner, who was a collector, died. The son loved the book so much he wouldn't be parted from it and took it to school with him. But he was a careless, thoughtless boy and covered the pages with scribbles and drawings. The book was soon tattered and dirty. One of his friends saw the book and was taken with the illustrations and their titles and asked if he could borrow it. The boy, who was generous by nature, gave it to his friend as a gift. The new owner treated the book quite differently. He cleaned the book up as much as he could, erased the drawings, kept it on his desk and treated it as his favourite. It was in his house that I saw the book for the first time. It was lying open at an illustration of pirates dividing up their booty. I was taken with that picture. We were rehearsing a play called* The Snow Queen *and I had a walk-on as one of a band of brigands. That picture would obviously be a great help to me with my costume and make-up. I asked if I could borrow the book for a few days so I could show it to the director and the rest of the cast. That's how I come to have it.*

Creating the Before-time in a Play

In the mid-1930s Stanislavski's wife, Lilina, worked on *The Cherry Orchard*.

At the opening of the play Madame Ranevskaya is returning to Russia after a long stay in Paris. She is accompanied by her daughter, Anya; the governess, Carlotta; and her manservant, Yasha. Her daughter Varya goes to the station to meet her from the midnight train, together with Ranevskaya's brother, Gaev; and a family friend, Pishchik. Lopakhin, a rich businessman; Dunyasha, the maid; and her admirer, Epikhodov, are waiting at the house.

Lilina worked out Varya's **Before-time** for Act One. Note that it is expressed in the first person and the present tense.

STUDIO NOTES

Varya:

1. I am in the carriage on my way to the station to meet my mother and am giving some final instructions to Dunyasha (to prepare mother's and Anya's rooms, to make coffee etc.).

2. I tell the coachman to hurry because I am afraid of being late to meet the train (although I have left early).

3. I see the station and throw off the travelling rug practically before we stop and jump out.

4. I run into the station. I look for someone on duty and run and ask him whether the train has arrived (although I know it's not yet 12.00, but better to check).

5. I go on to the platform alone and wait.

6. I hear a whistle in the distance. I watch the station doors: are the others coming? . . . I watch the incoming train from afar. They've all finally arrived. All my attention is on the train. I send Pishchik to the other end of the platform. I look through the windows of the incoming train. The train stops. I watch the passengers as they get off, they're not there . . . it can't be this train.

7. I run to the stationmaster to try to find out what has happened. Our train should have arrived but it hasn't.

8. I wait. The stationmaster is talking on the line. I listen, trying not to miss a single word. I learn that the international train is two hours late.

9. I go back to the rest. They are all in the station buffet. I tell them the train is late.

10. I sit in the buffet, but I don't drink tea, I listen to Gaev and Pishchik talking. From time to time I go out on to the platform and listen to every rumble and whistle.

11. I hear the whistle . . . I fetch everyone. I string them out along the platform, I watch the incoming train.

12. The train approaches the platform. I watch every carriage window as it flashes past. I know . . . it's them, I can see familiar faces in the window.

13. I run along with the moving train to that window. The train stops. I dash to it, I wait my turn to say hello, trying to see how my mother is. I greet her, trying to hide my emotion.

14. I attend to the unloading and loading of the luggage.

15. I help my mother and Anya into the carriage. I hug them warmly.

16. I go in the small carriage with Carlotta, Pishchik and Yasha. I put the hatbox on my knees.

17. I think about Mother the whole way. I think about ways of making Mother really comfortable at home. I exchange the odd word with Carlotta and Pishchik. I watch Mother's carriage the whole time.

18. We arrive. I get out of the carriage quickly. I ask Dunyasha if everything is in order. I send her to fetch the older servants so they can offer bread and salt.

19. I help Mother down from the carriage.

20. I give orders about unloading everything and put Epikhodov and Yasha in charge while I join Mother and go with her to her room.

Often a play, or a scene, opens at a high emotional level with no preparation. This is particularly true of Shakespeare. Only a full knowledge of the **Before-time** enables actors to get into the scene with genuine feeling, not just pulling 'emotion' out of the air.

In 1930, Stanislavski worked on his production plan for *Othello*. The play opens with Rodrigo and Iago, who enters in a state of high emotion.

Iago is the key to the plot. It is he who sets the tragedy in motion. But why? Shakespeare only tells us that he resents being passed over as Othello's second in command for Michael Cassio. Then there is the bald statement in Act I, scene iii, 'I hate the Moor.' and his suspicion that Othello has slept with his wife, Emilia:

> And it is thought abroad that 'twixt my sheets
> He has done my office . . .

That is all.

Stanislavski realised that the only solution to the problem was to create a detailed **Before-time** for the actor so that he could launch into the play.

Having described the way in which Iago met and began to use the gullible Rodrigo, Stanislavski provided the actor with the following biographical sketch for Iago:

From Stanislavski's 1930 *Othello* production plan†
Iago's past.

He rose from the ranks. On the outside he is hail-fellow-well-met, open, loyal. He is a brave soldier. He has been at Othello's side in all his battles and once saved his life. He is intelligent, wily. He understands perfectly Othello's tactics in war which he developed thanks to his military skill and his intuition. Othello regularly consults Iago before and during battle and Iago has often given him intelligent and useful advice. He is two men: the one others see, the other, the man he really is; one friendly, simple, generous hearted, the other evil and repulsive. The mask he has assumed hides him to such an extent that everyone (and to a certain degree his wife) takes him for the simplest, most guileless of men. If Desdemona had had a black child, he would have had this great, rough but kind-hearted man to care for it instead of a nurse. The child would also probably have had this wolf in sheep's clothing as his tutor. This is how Othello sees Iago although he has seen his audacity and his cruelty in war. He knows that in battle men become beasts, himself included. However, this does not prevent him from being gentle, feeling, almost shy. Moreover, Othello appreciates Iago's intelligence and wiliness highly. Iago has often given him good advice in battle. In the camp, Iago has been not only his adviser but his friend. Othello confided his disappointments, his doubts, his hopes to him. Iago always slept in Othello's tent. On sleepless nights, the great general would open up

† *Rezhisiorskij Plan 'Otello'* (Iskusstvo, Moscow, 1945), pp. 13–18.

his heart. Iago was his valet, his maid and, when necessary, his doctor. No one knew better than he how to dress a wound and, when necessary, give encouragement, or strike up a filthy but funny song or tell a good story. People excused him because he was such a good fellow. Many times Iago's songs and cynical stories were a blessing. For example, when the men were tired and fractious, along would come Iago with his songs and his cynical stories and the mood changed. At other times, when something was needed to satisfy the embittered soldiers, Iago did not hesitate to devise a form of torture or savage execution for a prisoner to delight the angry men. Of course, Othello knew nothing of this, the noble Moor did not allow torture. When necessary, he would strike off someone's head with a single blow.

Iago is honest. He doesn't steal money or goods. He is too intelligent to run any risks. But if he can deceive a fool (and there are many of them, apart from Rodrigo) he doesn't miss the opportunity. He takes anything from them: money, gifts, invitations, women, horses, pups etc. This additional money enables him to lead a riotous life. Emilia knows nothing of this although, perhaps, she guesses. Iago's closeness to Othello, the fact that he has risen from the ranks, that he sleeps in Othello's tent, that he is Othello's right arm etc., naturally arouses jealousy in the other officers and affection in the ranks. But everyone is afraid of him and respects him, for he is a real, an ideal soldier, a man of war who has very often got them out of trouble or averted a catastrophe. Military life suits him.

But Iago is out of place in Venice with its brilliance, its formality, the grand receptions which dignitaries offer and which Othello has to attend. Besides which, the general is not a man of culture and learning. He needs someone at his side who can make up for what he lacks, an aide who can be entrusted with a commission to the Doge or the senators. He needs someone who can write a letter or explain to him a military theory which he does not understand. Would Iago be able to do that? Of course, Cassio, who is educated, is much more suitable. Cassio is Florentine, and at that time the Florentines were like the Parisians of today, the epitome of elegance and sophistication. How could Iago take a message to Brabantio or arrange a secret rendezvous with Desdemona? Only

Cassio can undertake such errands. Small wonder then, that Othello has made him his lieutenant or, so to speak, his aide-de-camp. Moreover, the Moor never once thought of Iago as a possible candidate. Why should he need such a post? He is already an intimate, one of the family, a friend. Let him stay that way. Why put an uneducated, uncouth man in a ridiculous situation which would make him a figure of fun? This is what Othello thought.

But Iago thought otherwise. After all his service, his courage and bravery, saving the general's life more than once, his friendship, his devotion, only he, and no one else, could be the general's aide-de-camp. He would not have minded so much if someone of eminence, or someone among his comrades-in-arms, had been appointed, but to take the first pretty young officer who came along and who knew nothing of war! To choose this baby because he can read and knows how to talk to the ladies and bow and scrape to the great of this world – Iago cannot understand the general's logic. Cassio's appointment is, therefore, a blow to him, an outrage, a humiliation, an insult he cannot forgive. Even worse is the fact that he was never even considered. But the final blow is that Othello hid his most intimate, deepest concerns – his love for Desdemona and the abduction from him and confided all to the boy Cassio. Small wonder then that since Cassio's appointment as Othello's aide-de-camp, Iago has been drowning his sorrows. It was perhaps during one of these drinking bouts that he met and became friends with Rodrigo. Their favourite topics in his nocturnal conversations with his new friend were, on the one hand, Rodrigo's dream that Iago will arrange to carry off Desdemona and, on the other, Iago's complaints about the way the general has behaved. To fuel the flames of their rancour, they go back over everything, Iago's merits and Othello's ingratitude which had not been apparent earlier but which now seem quite criminal. They remember stories about Emilia that were current in the army.

In fact, when Iago was Othello's close friend, there had been stories. To cheer themselves up, the troops had decided all sorts of reasons for Iago's close friendship with the general. One of the reasons given was that something had been going on and was still going on between Othello and Emilia. Naturally, they made sure that Iago got to hear of it. But he did not pay it much attention:

first, because he never bothered much about Emilia and deceived her; second, because he had no special feeling for her. He liked her plump figure, she was a good housewife, she could sing and play the lute, she was cheerful, she might have a little money, coming from a good merchant family, and she was well brought up for the period. If there had been something between them (and he knew then that there was nothing) he would not have been very upset. But now, having been cruelly insulted, he remembers the stories about Emilia. He would like, he needs there to be something between her and the general. That would justify his hate, his desire for vengeance. Now Iago wants to justify these rumours because they are in fact lies. Emilia gets on well with Othello. He is famous, kind, lonely, with no one to look after him, his quarters lack a woman's touch, and so this good housewife comes and tidies the bachelor general's house. Iago knows that. He has met her in Othello's rooms and never paid attention to it, but now he blames her for it. In a word, Iago deludes himself into believing something that never happened. This gives him the pretext to rage, to accuse and condemn a guiltless Othello, and to stir up his malice and bile. It was in these circumstances that Iago learnt of something amazing, unexpected, incomprehensible: the abduction of Desdemona. He could not believe his eyes when he went into the general's quarters and saw this painted beauty practically embracing the Moor, who for him now has become a black devil. The blow was so great that his brain almost seizes up. When he learns how he, a close friend, had been kept in the dark by the lovers, under Cassio's guidance, and when he hears happy voices laughing at him, he runs away to hide the rage that boils up inside him.

The abduction of Desdemona has not only hurt him but has also put him in a totally ridiculous position with Rodrigo. While fleecing him, Iago continuously promised to obtain his beauty, by kidnapping her if need be, if Brabantio did not give his agreement. Now even the simpleton Rodrigo has understood that Iago has duped him. Is Iago really close to the general? Rodrigo no longer believes in his friendship. In a word, their relationship is ended. Rodrigo is angry, like a stupid, obstinate child. For the moment, he forgets that Iago saved him from a beating by drunkards.

When Iago learns what has happened he decides not to give up.

He believes that all is not lost and that if a scandal were created throughout the city, then Othello would be in a bad position and that, perhaps, the marriage might be dissolved by higher authority. He is right, of course. This is probably what would have happened were it not for the war. The government need Othello too much for them to annul his marriage at such a critical moment.

Until war breaks out, Iago is right to try to annul the marriage.

There is no time to be lost. When action is required, Iago acts with diabolical energy. He covers all possibilities. He goes back to the newly married couple, congratulates them, laughs with them, calls himself a fool. He manages to persuade Desdemona that only jealousy for his beloved general made him behave so stupidly when he learned of the marriage. Then he hurries to see Rodrigo. When Rodrigo learned what had happened, the poor fool first wept like a child, then swore at his friend and decided their friendship was over. Iago has great difficulty in explaining his plan: to create a scandal, stir up the whole city and obtain a divorce or an annulment. We meet the two friends at the moment when Iago has practically forced Rodrigo into a gondola and taken him to Brabantio's house. They have arrived. The gondolier steps on to dry land, attaches the boat and waits.

They must begin but Rodrigo is still obstinate and hardly says a word to Iago.

Rodrigo is very, very angry with Iago. Iago is very, very perplexed and tries to repair the damage. First, because Rodrigo is his purse and second, because he needs him today to rouse the whole city. There is no time to be lost, otherwise the wedding night will have passed and the situation will be irreparable.

THE SUBTEXT

In life, action and thought are simultaneous. The mind is continually active (even while the body, apparently, is not, as when we are asleep). In a play, this mental activity has to be created for each character. It has two aspects:

1. The thoughts that go through our mind, the **Inner Monologue**.

2. The pictures we see in our mind, our **Mental Images**.

Both occur spontaneously in our daily lives but have to be consciously created in the theatre.

The Inner Monologue

This occurs:

> When we are listening to someone else speaking.
> When there is a pause in our own speech.
> When we have to create mentally what we are reading, or hearing – say, on the telephone.

STUDIO NOTES

A student is asked to imagine she is a paediatrician in a country hospital.

Situation: The emergency department has just closed. That evening she is going to the theatre.

Action: The day's work has just ended. She clears away the patients' medical records from the table. She tidies herself up and puts on another pair of shoes. She transfers her theatre tickets and opera-glasses from a large bag to a small evening bag. She consults the clock. She quickly puts on her coat, switches off the light and goes to the door. Suddenly the telephone rings. She hesitates. Shall she take the call or not? She decides she will and lifts the receiver. 'Emergency. Yes. [She lights the table lamp.] Address. [She writes it down.] I'll be with you right away.' She gets her medical bag and puts in instruments, medication. She puts on her doctor's coat, changes shoes, switches off the light and leaves in a hurry.

Inner Monologue*: What was being said to her on the other end of the line?*

A woman said that her child had fallen down the stairs, was badly hurt and she needed help quickly.

Question: Did she write down a real address or just make a few squiggles on the paper?

In a play the author provides the dialogue, the things we say, but we need to create the **Inner Monologue**, the thoughts that lie behind them.

STUDIO NOTES
Stanislavski took a scene between Varya and Lopakhin in the last act of The Cherry Orchard.

Varya is in love with Lopakhin. The family hopes he will marry her and so assure her future and he has promised to do so. This is the last opportunity for him to propose before the family leaves their home forever. They tactfully leave them alone. Varya finds excuses to stay in the room, in the hope he will say something.

VARYA *(taking a long look at everything)* Strange, I can't find it anywhere . . .

LOPAKHIN What are you looking for?

VARYA I put it down and now I don't know where.
Pause.

LOPAKHIN Where will you go now?

VARYA To the Ragulins. I've agreed to run their house . . . a sort of housekeeper.

LOPAKHIN That's in Yashnievo, isn't it? About fifty miles away. *(Pause.)* So, your life is over in this house.

VARYA *(looking at the luggage)* Where can it be . . . Or perhaps I put it in the trunk . . . Yes, my life here is over . . . there's no future now.

LOPAKHIN I'm just off to Kharkov . . . by the same train. I've a great deal to do. I'm leaving Epikhodov here. I've taken him on.

VARYA Really!

LOPAKHIN This time last year, if you remember, it was already snowing, but now there's sun and not a breath of wind. But it *is* cold . . . Three degrees below zero.

VARYA I didn't look. *(Pause.)* And then our thermometer's broken.
Pause.

A voice from the courtyard door: 'Lopakhin!'

LOPAKHIN *(As though he had been waiting to be called for some time)* Coming right away! *(Exits quickly.)*

Varya sits on the floor, puts her head on a bundle and quietly sobs.

Stanislavski imagined Varya's **Inner Monologue**, *as follows:*

Now he'll finally propose to me. What happiness that will be! What's the matter with him? What's he about? He's embarrassed, he doesn't know how

to begin! Pluck up courage, I'll wait . . . Dear God! Still talking about
something else. Did mother . . . No, No, he'll say it now . . . everything will
be all right. Speak quickly, my dear! . . . He still doesn't . . . Did mother
make it all up? It can't be true! No, no . . . He's gone . . . it's all over . . .
forever!

Mental Images

If I say, 'I am going home,' I know what 'home' is like, I can
visualise it, I can describe it to others in great detail. My
statement is informed by my knowledge of the place where I live
and the pictures which are automatically in my head when I
speak of it. But if I am given 'I am going home' as a line of
dialogue, what is that 'home'? It doesn't exist and cannot exist
unless I imagine it or unless the designer creates it for me. And
even then, I will have to make that designer's 'home' my own,
know what it feels like to live there, I will need to see myself
moving through it. It will have to be present in my mind while
I am on stage talking about it. And what about the rooms the
designer doesn't show? I need to create a sequence of **Mental
Images** in which I can see myself at home. Stanislavski
compared this to making a film which I can then run in my
head, as if on a mental screen, any time I like. The more often
I run the film, the more familiar it becomes, it becomes habit,
as familiar actions do in life.

My **Mental Images**, my 'film', have to be communicated
to other actors. While I am doing the exercises the group can
ask questions which will lead to more detailed answers and
descriptions until a complete, detailed film has been created,
which can be re-run at will.

Studio Exercises
Use real events.
■ Remember coming to class today, or going from your house to
   the railway station, or any other familiar journey. Describe it,
   indicating any special features, any landmarks along the way.
■ Describe your home (room, flat, house). The rest of the group
   should be able to make a ground-plan, showing the layout of

the room(s) and the furniture.
- ■ Describe a well-known building in your town or city without saying what it is, so that the group can name it.
- ■ Describe a statue, a monument, a well-known painting.
- ■ Take a reproduction of a painting or a photograph and give it to two or three students to study for thirty to forty seconds. They must then describe it in detail to the others who have to reproduce the picture from the description. Compare what they have done with the original.

Use imaginary events.
- ■ Create situations in which you are a stationary observer. Use **What 'if'. . . ?**

What if I were:
- • A tree?
- • A traffic cop?
- • A look-out on a tower?

Where am I? What do I see? What do I hear? When is this happening? What is the reason for my being here? Etc.
- ■ You are shopping in an imaginary department store.*

Describe the layout of the store, the objects on display, how you get from floor to floor.

EMOTION MEMORY

In Part One we recognised that the only emotions we can feel in the situation the writer has invented are our own. The process of defining and carrying out precise physical actions with the thoughts and images that accompany them automatically produces feelings and emotions, but they may not be deep enough or full enough for what the scene requires. We then need consciously to draw on our own life experiences. The ability, the skill to recall past experiences, physical and mental, **Emotion Memory**, is one of our richest sources of material.†

† *A word of caution*: Some memories, often painful ones, have been deliberately suppressed by the mind, because we have not found ways of dealing with or coming to terms with the experience. Don't, in Stanislavski's words, 'assault the subconscious'. Our deepest feelings have to be lured, enticed, not forced. *Rehearsal is not group therapy. Acting is not analysis.*

The nature of memory is still a matter of scientific investigation, not least because it seems so arbitrary. Some things we remember, others we forget and the harder we try the more they elude us. Sometimes we resort to rhymes, little poems and other mnemonics to recall essential facts.

The physiological base of memory is being established but its functioning, how we remember, is not. There are reasonable grounds for assuming that everything we have felt and experienced is recorded somewhere in the brain. From our own experience we know that memories appear to be linked.

If someone asks me if I would like a coffee, I recall a general sense of what coffee tastes like, before answering. I then recall different kinds of coffee I could have – instant, espresso, cappuccino, American, Turkish – and in each case I recall a special flavour.

If I am asked what I am going to do for Christmas, my reaction is much more complex. First, perhaps, I have a 'Christmas' feeling, a general sense of well-being and pleasure, representing all the Christmases I have spent. This general mood will then, if I think further, separate out into different Christmases with particular features, special presents, meals, amusing incidents, absent friends or relatives. I begin to recall specific years in detail and begin to experience again the feelings I had at the time. Depending on the circumstances, my feelings can be very strong.

This is a natural process and presents no difficulties. Unfortunately, memory is very fickle. I can't access it at will. It is not like clicking the mouse on my personal computer to access a file. The job of acting would be simpler if I could. Memory cannot be forced. If I forget a telephone number, the harder I try to remember it the more elusive it becomes. I block myself by my own effort. But it will come into my head, perhaps, later, when I am not thinking about it and am doing something else.

If I can't control my memory completely, I can train myself to use it better. Like any other skill, recall can be improved. I can also build up a repertoire of memories which I can access quickly in rehearsal or when working on a role. The quicker I can access my own experiences, the fewer the barriers to the flow of my creative process. This is basic groundwork that I can do at home, as well as in class.

Recurrent Emotion

Most of the feelings which we experience are, in fact, feelings which we have experienced before, or which are similar, they are *recurrent* emotions. We do not often have a completely new, first-time or *primary* emotion. In acting we mainly use recurrent emotions. If things go well in rehearsal, these feelings will arise naturally out of our actions. But if they don't, we need a technique to access what is in our memories.

If our minds were just like computers and our memories like computer memory, there would be no problem. The computer manual tells us what to do: click the mouse on the right item on the right menu and the item will appear. Unfortunately, we don't have any such manual or a mouse for accessing our own memories. We can, however, develop our capacity to remember, and build up a readily available store of memories.

Developing Emotion Memory

We can work on developing **Emotion Memory** in three phases, by studying:
1. sensory memory (the memory of our five senses)
2. memory of past experiences
3. triggers, or ways of gently jogging our memory, without trying to force what is hidden out into the open.

Sensory Memory

There are two aspects to sensory memory, physical and mental.

When I say, ' I remember the taste of an apple,' the idea of an apple comes into my mind, then I recall the taste.

Our memory does not function equally well with all five senses in all of us. For some, visual memory is dominant, for others, hearing etc. Some exercises will, therefore, be easy and others difficult. Work on those you find difficult.

The Five Senses

STUDIO EXERCISES

The object is to recall actual experience. If any of the exercises falls outside your own experience, ignore it, don't try to imagine it. Recall may happen easily. If it doesn't, try to remember the circumstances in which the experience occurred in as much detail as possible. If you still have difficulty, leave that particular exercise and go on to another. As your skill develops, you will find that you can go back to exercises that were once difficult and are now much easier.

Sight: Picture the following:
■ A house you have visited or where you once lived.
■ An elephant, a camel, a dog, a cat, an earthworm.
■ A wasp, a bee, a moth, a beetle, a ladybird.
■ A centipede, a caterpillar.
■ A starry sky, the moon.
■ One of the most famous buildings in your city.
■ Winter snow, ice, mist.

Sound: Hear the following:
■ The sound of waves breaking on the shore.
■ The wind rattling the window.
■ The dripping of raindrops.
■ A piano, a guitar, a trumpet.
■ A dog barking.
■ Chopping wood, sawing wood.
■ The cawing of a crow, the chirping of a sparrow.
■ The buzzing of a bee.
■ Heavy lorries on a road, a motorcycle.
■ The shunting of trains into a siding.
■ Feet crunching in the snow.
■ Footsteps climbing stairs.
■ Trees moving in the wind.
■ An orchestra tuning up etc.
■ A jet plane, a helicopter.*

Smell: Smell the following:
- The sea.
- Roses, lilac, jasmine, hyacinth, honeysuckle.
- A grilled steak, hot toast, curry.*
- Petrol, wine, coffee, tea.
- Smoke from a wood fire, rain on wet grass.
- An apple, an orange etc.

Taste: Taste in your mouth:
- Chocolate, ice-cream.
- An apple, an orange, a lemon, raspberries.
- Roast beef, fried chicken.*
- Jam, butter, honey, grapefruit juice etc.*

Touch: Imagine the feel of:
- Putting your hands into hot, tepid, cold water.
- Stroking a cat, a dog.
- The texture of cotton, wool, silk, velvet, sandpaper.
- Taking a hot shower, towelling off, putting on a cool cotton shirt/blouse.*
- Trying to do up buttons with freezing cold fingers.*
- Hot tea on your tongue.
- The surface of a pineapple, a cabbage, a wet fish etc.

EXERCISES: THE FIVE SENSES COMBINED
- Imagine you are taking a familiar journey – to a shop, the local railway station, school. Remember and try to experience everything you see, hear, smell, taste, touch on the way. Do not invent. Take the time you need actually to recall each sensation.

Memory of Past Experiences

The memory may come quickly, without much effort. Again, if it doesn't, don't try to force it but recall the circumstances in which the feeling arose until the feeling comes to life. If you have problems, pass on to another exercise and come back later.

STUDIO EXERCISES
(Note: Keep the memories simple, don't go after something obviously 'theatrical' or 'dramatic'.)
Recall:
- An enjoyable party.
- Something disagreeable.
- Something that made you angry.
- When you had a success.
- When you felt ashamed.
- When you received some good news.
- When you were told a secret.
- When you envied someone.
- When you experienced curiosity.
- When you gossiped about someone.
- When you were bored.
- When you deceived someone, they deceived you.
- When you felt depressed.
- When you felt terrified.
- When you had to run away from someone.
- When you recovered from an illness.
- When you quarrelled with family and friends.
- When you were given a present.
- When you bought a present for a friend.
- When you experienced grief over the death of someone close, or an animal.
- When you met someone you didn't like.
- When you were waiting at home for a friend to arrive.
- When you learned a friend was ill.
- When you learned a slight acquaintance was ill etc.

Using Memory Triggers and Improvisations in Rehearsal

In rehearsal, **Emotion Memories** may come spontaneously and pass straight into the performance as part of the emotional experience of the character, not just as part of your personal memory. If they do not, then two preliminary phases need to be gone through:

1. Recall a moment in your life when you experienced an emotion analogous to that which the character is experiencing – the 'then'.
2. Improvise in the present a situation which will provoke the same emotion – the 'now'.

Then rehearse the scene with these experiences in mind.

By this process the past is brought into the present and made immediate but in an imaginary situation, so that distance is created between us and our memories. They then become material out of which a character can be shaped.

STUDIO NOTES
The scene in rehearsal is one in which your character experiences terror.
1. As in the exercises above, recall an occasion when you experienced terror. The 'then'. A friend and I were going through a public park at night with heavy bags full of shopping. It was very dark, eerie, there wasn't a soul about. Suddenly we became aware that we could see someone stealing through the bushes. We were scared, we stopped and looked at each other. The noise of movement continued. We didn't exchange a word but communicated in gestures. We tried moving on tiptoe without making a sound, hoping we wouldn't tread on any dried twigs and give ourselves away. We kept looking round and trying to hear if we were being followed. When we'd put a decent distance between ourselves and whoever it was we took to our heels and ran and didn't stop until we were out of the park.
2. Improvisation. The 'now'.
I am alone with my sister / brother. It is late at night. The doorbell rings. I go to the door and ask who is there. No reply. But I can feel that there is someone outside. I put the security chain on the door and open it. There is a tall man with a bunch of keys in his hand. I shut the door and ask once again what he wants. No answer. I bolt the door and with my sister / brother push heavy furniture against it. We wait. After a while I put my ear to the door and listen. Silence. I cautiously open the door with the chain still on. No one there.

Let us apply this technique to a specific scene, *Macbeth* Act II, scene ii, using the Studio example, with terror as the dominant emotion. Repeat both phases from your own experience. Then work on the scene.

Macbeth enters with his hands covered with blood, having murdered King Duncan as he slept. Lady Macbeth is waiting:

MACBETH

I have done the deed. Didst thou not hear a noise?

LADY MACBETH

I heard the owl scream and the crickets cry.

Did not you speak?

MACBETH   When?

LADY MACBETH   Now.

MACBETH   As I descended?

LADY MACBETH

Ay.

MACBETH   Hark! – Who lies i' th' second chamber?

LADY MACBETH

Donalbain.

This is a highly charged scene which may require further exercises and improvisations in sensory memory (e.g. frightening sounds, being in the pitch dark) and memory of past experience (e.g. being afraid of the dark, being trapped in a confined space) before the right level of intensity can be naturally achieved. If you experience a difficulty or a block at any stage, go through more 'then' and 'now' exercises before returning to the play. Do not attempt to play 'terror'.

EXERCISE

Find examples of short scenes from other plays you know where the dramatic situation creates a dominant emotion (fear, joy, sadness) and repeat the process of 'then' and 'now' before rehearsing it. Again, do not try to go directly to the emotion. Allow your memories of physical sensations and past experiences to encourage the emotion to appear. If you have problems, explore the situation and **Emotion Memory** further.

Mind and Body

Although for the convenience of study we treat them separately, mind and body cannot be split. They form a continuum.

These classes study:

The influence of mental states on physical behaviour
The influence of physical states on mental behaviour
The influence of our surroundings on behaviour
The influence of external stimuli on behaviour

THE INFLUENCE OF MENTAL STATES ON PHYSICAL BEHAVIOUR

A mental state can produce a physical state. Sometimes we see someone walking down the street smiling. They are thinking about something that makes them happy but are unaware of their own facial expression.

STUDIO EXERCISES

It is essential only to concentrate on the inner, mental state, and to experience it fully. *Do not give out deliberate physical signs, or send 'signals'*. That would destroy the whole purpose of the exercises, which is to allow inner feeling to express itself in ways you may not be aware of.

■ Each student in turn goes out of the room, thinks of something which makes them happy, or sad, or angry etc., and returns. The rest of the group observe the student's behaviour and define the mood they are in.*

■ Each student imagines they are reading a book. The rest of the group try to determine, from their observation of the student, what kind of book it is.*

■ Each student imagines a situation in which they are waiting

for something, good news, bad news, to have a tooth out etc.
The student simply sits on a chair. The rest of the group must
try to determine what kind of situation it is.*

THE INFLUENCE OF PHYSICAL STATES ON MENTAL BEHAVIOUR

Conversely, physical states can produce mental states. For
example, in some people the absence of sunshine in winter
months produces clinical depression or Seasonal Affective
Disorder (SAD). There are cases in which extreme physical
assault has so traumatised the victims that although they are
physically capable, they are unable to speak and describe their
assailant.

We must define the character's physical state very precisely.
It must be specific to the scene on each occasion and not just a
series of token gestures. To yawn and stretch to indicate you
have just woken up, no matter what the play, is a meaningless
cliché.

Let us look at a couple of examples of physical exhaustion,
tiredness, in our own experience.

EXAMPLES:
What is the longest, most tiring, most uncomfortable journey you
have ever taken? (Never mind the means of transport.)*
■ Improvise a similar journey, making the situation quite
   specific. For example, you are on holiday on a remote island.
   Your family calls you home urgently. The journey is 500
   miles.*
When have you run until you dropped to get somewhere in time?
■ Improvise a situation in which you have to catch a train.
   There are no taxis or buses. You have to run fast, with your
   suitcase, if you don't want to miss it. You fall into the carriage
   at the very last minute.*
In each case, which parts of you are the most tired, hurt the most
(physical state)? How does that affect your mood (mental state)?
What are the differences in the quality of the tiredness between
the two examples?

Let us now take three examples of physical exhaustion, in three different plays.

1. In Act One of *The Cherry Orchard*, Irina returns home to Russia. She has come by train from Paris and has not slept properly for two or three days. By the end of the act she has fallen asleep in mid-conversation.

2. At the end of *A Midsummer Night's Dream*, a terrified Hermia has been running through the wood.

HERMIA
   Never so weary, never so in woe,
   I can no further crawl, no further go.
      My legs can keep no pace with my desires [. . .]
   Here will I rest me till the break of day.

3. In Arthur Miller's *Death of a Salesman*, Willy Loman, the central character, returns home after an exhausting and frustrating sales trip, and describes how he lost concentration and nearly drove off the road.

In all three cases we can define the physical state as 'exhaustion', but the precise nature of the 'exhaustion', and the actions and language which express it, differ in form and quality according to the situation the character is in and, of course, to the **Before-time**.

We may need to do 'then' exercises on various examples of our sense memories, say, of different moments of 'exhaustion', to find the most appropriate, and then to do 'now' improvisations to experience that specific 'exhaustion' in an imaginary situation.

At the Studio, Stanislavski took as an example the effect of drunkenness on behaviour.

STUDIO NOTES
In class, Stanislavski gave the example of Lopakhin in The Cherry Orchard *who in Act Three is both emotionally and physically 'high'. He returns from the auction, having purchased the cherry orchard. He is drunk with joy, excited, triumphant (mental state): he, the starved, beaten, barefoot peasant boy, has finally 'made it', he has bought the estate on which his*

family were less than the hired help, mere serfs. But, more important, he is also just plain drunk (physical state) and that marks his entire behaviour.

Oblivious to the pain he is causing Ranevskaya, who treated him with kindness as a boy, dried his tears and washed his face after he had been beaten by his father, he exults in his victory, he laughs, he dances. Then, when he sees Ranevskaya weeping, he suddenly remembers what it means to her and expresses his profound sympathy:

> LOPAKHIN   Why, oh why didn't you listen to me? Poor lady, dear good lady, there's no going back now. (*He weeps.*) Oh, if only this could all be over and something could change in our stupid, unhappy lives, and quickly.

But the moment of sobriety is past and he reverts to his state of drunken triumph.

> LOPAKHIN   Let's have some decent music. Things must be the way I want them! (*He bumps into a table and nearly knocks over a candlestick.*) I can pay for anything!

How differently would Lopakhin have behaved had he been triumphant but sober?

THE INFLUENCE OF OUR SURROUNDINGS ON BEHAVIOUR

Our mental state is influenced by our surroundings and the stimuli they provide, which spontaneously evoke memories of past experiences.

EXERCISE

■ Arrange chairs in such a way that none are facing each other and some are back to back. The group selects a theme for improvisation.

They go out of the room for a while, return and sit on the chairs and try to work out the details of the improvisation, the circumstances etc.

Can there be a useful discussion with the chairs set in that pattern? Do you feel at ease?

Rearrange the chairs until you can communicate properly with each other.

THE INFLUENCE OF EXTERNAL STIMULI ON BEHAVIOUR

At the Studio, Stanislavski experimented with the effect light and sound produce on mood and atmosphere.

STUDIO NOTES

1. Sit comfortably so that the group can see each other. Exchange memories of Christmases you have spent, or summer holidays.

At first the room is brightly lit. Slowly the lights dim until there is only half-light. Moonlight comes through the window. After a while the lights suddenly come up to full.

What was the effect of the light changes on the atmosphere and the mood of each individual? Did the half-light make it easier for you to open up and share your experiences? How did you respond to the moonlight? Did the return to full light break your mood?

2. The group sits reading. The lights dim but one student is lit by a bright spotlight. The spotlight goes out and another student is spotlit.

What is the effect of suddenly being singled out?

3. The group are sitting, making notes, either recording the day's work and studio exercises or working out material for use the next day. They should concentrate fully on their activity.

The following sounds are heard in the next room or outside:

> *a cat miaowing*
> *a piano playing soft music*
> *hammering nails*
> *total silence*
> *a quarrel which increases in intensity*
> *a plane flying very low overhead*
> *a car repeatedly sounding its horn and other horns responding*
> *people laughing*
> *a series of explosions coming ever closer*
> *a baby crying*

Analyse the effect of each sound on your mood and your ability to work.

Interaction

In life we are in active contact and communication the whole time with objects, other people, or, if alone with our own thoughts, with ideas and feelings. We interact with others, we think about the world. Our life is always *about* something.

We have to produce similar behaviour in the theatre. We must always be in living contact with the world of the play and the people in it, the other characters, throughout the performance.

There have been complaints since the seventeenth century (at least) about actors who go dead when it is not their line but somebody else's, and who only come alive again when it is their turn to speak.

They do not seem to realise that they not only make it difficult for other actors to give energy to their lines but they also undercut themselves; they deprive themselves of the impetus they might receive by actively responding to what is being said to them and using it as a springboard for their next line.

The word 'dialogue' means what it says, words between two people.

If we observe two people in deep conversation, we can almost see the field of energy between and around them.

These classes study:

- The basic elements of communication
- The structure of an act of communication
- Modes of communication
- Adaptation

THE BASIC ELEMENTS OF COMMUNICATION

In any act of communication there must be:

Something to be communicated, a feeling, a thought, a wish.

An object with which to communicate.

A means of communication – speech, gesture, the eyes.

A way of communicating, a series of choices as to approach. You may have to adapt and make fresh choices according to the response you receive.

THE STRUCTURE OF ACTS OF COMMUNICATION

In life we can identify five stages in any act of communication:

1. Selecting the person to be communicated with – the **Object of Attention**.
2. Focusing on that person and attracting their attention.
3. Trying to see what state of mind or mood they are in, probing them with the eyes.
4. Conveying our thoughts, feelings, mental images in the best way we can, choosing our words carefully, using voice and gesture expressively, so that the **Object of Attention** not only sees and hears the externals of what we are doing, but enters into our world of experience and shares it.
5. Ending the act of communication.

STUDIO EXERCISES

■ Ask a small group of students to make an exact list of all the props that will be needed for an improvisation they are going to prepare. Take another student aside and tell him to go up to one of the group while the list is being discussed and ask to borrow some money, very discreetly, so that the others don't realise what is happening.

■ Select the person you need from the group, while he is still busy and **a**. give him a note, **b**. send him off on an errand, **c**. persuade him to be available to you all day. Do this without distracting the rest of the group.

■ Select two students. Ask one to set up an imaginary situation and improvise on it without telling the other what the situation is. The second observes the first, trying to understand what he is doing, and finally joins in, observing all of the other's behaviour and matching his own accordingly. This is all done in silence.

■ One student engages in an activity which requires the use of materials and perhaps tools, e.g. making a model, using cardboard, scissors, glue, clips. A second student observes for a while and then joins in, handing the first student whatever is required.*

■ On a given signal, two students spontaneously adopt a position in relation to each other. They each inwardly justify the position and then begin to move, observing each other, trying to understand and justify their actions. They decide what it is they are doing and coordinate and direct their efforts to a common end.

This last exercise was done at the Studio:

STUDIO NOTES
After moving and observing each other, the two students decided that their common goal was to go fishing.

They dragged a boat up on the shore, secured it to a mooring, put up a tent, made beds in it, collected firewood, made a fire etc.

The first student devised the situation and started to improvise on it and the second adapted to what he was doing.

MODES OF COMMUNICATION

There are several modes of communication, all of which we can develop.

Verbal

STUDIO EXERCISES
These are exercises in the careful and precise selection of words to meet a given situation.

■ You are a doctor. Your patient is lying in bed, heavily bandaged. Explain to the patient that he must not move.

■ Prison. Night. You are two in a cell. You are chained in

opposite corners. Explain who you are and where you have come from.

■ Your car has broken down. You are under it trying to repair it. Your companion is getting impatient and you ask him to help.

■ You are in the kitchen, your friend is in the dining-room. Discuss through the wall what you are going to eat.

■ Ring up the electrician and explain that your television set has broken down.*

■ Two people are engaged in conversation when the lights fail. Continue the conversation in the dark.

■ You are leaning out of the window on the fifth floor, relaying a shopping list to someone down in the street.

Gestural

STUDIO EXERCISES

There are occasions when words are denied us. We then resort to gesture. This is not mime, although there may be mimetic elements in it.

■ You are nursing a sleeping baby. Someone enters singing happily. Signal to him to keep quiet, that you have just got the baby to sleep with great difficulty and you'll be angry if it is woken up.

■ Arrange a meeting with your boyfriend/girlfriend through the window of their house.

■ You are in a library, or a lecture, where absolute silence is required. You and a friend are sitting in different parts of the room. Indicate very discreetly that you both have to leave because you have an appointment.

■ You are at a meeting at which decisions will be taken that will affect not only your own future but also that of your friends. The discussion has not gone the way you would have liked. You have one or two allies present. Try to organise them so that you can swing the meeting your way and even, if you can, indicate the order in which each of you should speak.

Mental

There are moments when we seem to communicate almost directly from mind to mind. Usually this occurs when looking into someone else's eyes.

Stanislavski called this 'radiation'. It was a process of transmitting and receiving rays, like radio. Two people act both as transmitter and receiver in a continuous exchange, during which there is the transmission and reception of thought and feeling.

What we may actually be doing is interpreting the minute adjustments of the facial muscles, which respond automatically to inner feelings without our knowing these adjustments are occurring.

What is important is the intention to communicate.

STUDIO EXERCISES
Working in pairs, try to 'transmit' feelings that result from
Emotion Memory:
■ Recall the death of a dear friend.
■ Recall the first time you quarrelled with your girlfriend/boyfriend.
■ Recall a happy and an unhappy occasion.
■ Contempt.
■ Pity.
■ Affection.
■ Antagonism.
■ Try to reach a common agreement.

When trying out these exercises it is essential not to 'do' anything, not to try consciously to adjust facial expression. That will lead to cliché and a kind of 'silent movie' acting.

The essential factor is the intensity of feeling you achieve by natural means i.e., by using the techniques of **Emotion Memory**.

ADAPTATION

In life, when we set out to do something, we rarely achieve our goal immediately. Since not everyone shares our intentions, indeed since they may be opposed to what we want, there are obstacles and conflicts along the way, which we have to overcome. We have, therefore, to vary our strategies, our approach, to use **Adaptations** to achieve our end.

In the Folio version, it takes Hamlet five hours to achieve his goal – avenging his father.

Let us re-examine the exercise described earlier (p. 77), in which a student went to a member of a group with a note etc., look at the adaptations and the use of various forms of communication.

Analysis:

The student first went up to the person (**Object of Attention**) he had selected, put a hand on his shoulder to get his attention (Gestural) and then looked at him intently (Mental). Then the **Object of Attention** moved a little so he could sit down beside him. He sat and passed the note, unobserved by the rest (Gestural). He sat for a while, made sure he had won the person's assent (Mental), and, after a while, looked at his watch, rose and left the room (Gestural).

In this version, the **Object of Attention** offers no resistance to what is being asked of him. But what if he needed persuading? What **Adaptations** would be necessary to achieve the desired end? What kinds of communication would they involve?

STUDIO EXERCISES

In each case change tactics (adapt) when you encounter resistance. Be obstinate until you succeed.

- There are two plays/films/concerts you could go to. Persuade an unwilling friend to go along with your choice.
- Find a way to get out of class early.
- Persuade a friend/relative to confide a secret to you.
- Today there is a rehearsal of one of your most important scenes. But you don't know your lines. Arrange it so that something else is rehearsed.

Tempo-rhythm

Music is held together by tempo and rhythm. Over a basic pulse, fast, medium, slow (tempo), notes of varying length are played and grouped to form a pattern (rhythm). This **Tempo-rhythm** produces an emotional effect – the difference between a funeral march and heavy rock.

In life, when two or more people are engaged in the same activity or job of work, a common tempo is either consciously or unconsciously established to promote efficiency. The most obvious example is the use of work-songs or shanties, which teams of men sing and so coordinate their efforts. This not only makes the work, which may be uncongenial, go smoothly, but it also makes the participants feel better.

These classes study:

Outer tempo-rhythm
The influence of outer tempo-rhythm on mental states
Inner tempo-rhythm
The influence of mental states on outer tempo-rhythm
Contradictory inner and outer tempo-rhythms
Varying tempo-rhythms

OUTER TEMPO-RHYTHM

Conduct an experiment: Observe the person working at a supermarket checkout, the way he/she processes all the items, the kind of tempo established, the varying rhythms used when dealing with different objects. When it is your turn, try to fall in with the **Tempo-rhythm** of the checkout as you put your purchases into a plastic bag and see if you can maintain the **Tempo-rhythm** by having your money/cheque/credit card ready as the total cost comes up on the screen.

In the theatre, sequences of actions, scenes, gain from being played at an appropriate tempo with the right rhythmic patterns. The unity and consistency of both tempo and rhythm make it easier for the audience to follow the action. At the same time, they are emotionally affected by it.

We need to make ourselves sensitive to the nature of **Tempo-rhythm**, and learn to use it creatively.

We need to look at:

Tempo: the speed of the basic pulse.

Rhythm: the relationship of movement and stillness in time and space.

Bar: a segment of time, counted in beats – a march has two beats to a bar, a waltz, three.

Metre: a dominant, recurring rhythmic pattern, as in certain dances.

In the exercises we shall mainly work with four beats in a bar – 4/4.

There can be:

One note to a bar, lasting four beats.

Two notes to a bar, lasting two beats each.

Four notes to a bar, lasting one beat each.

And so on up to thirty-two notes or more, so that one bar could be made up of $1/4 + 2/16 + 4/32 + 4/8$.

STUDIO EXERCISES

This sequence of exercises is designed to develop a physical awareness of rhythm.

■ Clapping.

Divide into 4 groups. Group 1 claps one beat to a bar, establishing a basic pulse (tempo). The other groups join in succession. Group 2, two beats to a bar. Group 3, four to a bar. Group 4, eight to a bar.

Repeat the exercise in varying tempos.

■ Walking.

In a bar of four beats walk successively one step, two steps, four steps, eight steps to a bar. Take time to experience the different quality of each rate of walking.

Switch rhythms so that they contrast. Go from eight steps to a bar to one step to a bar, then four steps to a bar etc.

■ Hands.

In varying rhythms:

- Shake water from your hands.
- Extend your fingers, singly, as a whole.
- Curl each finger in turn.
- Draw a figure of eight in the air.
- Pass an object from one to another.

■ Simple Actions.

In varying rhythms perform any or all of the following, or similar actions:

- Dust the furniture.
- Clean the windows.
- Turn over the pages in a book.
- Count the number of matches in a box.
- Put books and papers into a briefcase.
- Find a letter in an untidy drawer.

Initially, everyone works to the same rhythm. Then work individually, changing rhythm frequently.

In some of these exercises (walking and hands) a metronome can be useful to establish the pattern of activity. Later, the metronome should be taken away.

THE INFLUENCE OF OUTER TEMPO-RHYTHM ON MENTAL STATES

STUDIO EXERCISES

■ Actions (in bars of 4/4). Fix the tempo.

1. Pick up a book – 2 beats. Open it – 2 beats.
2. Read a page – 4 beats.
3. Turn the page – 1 beat, read 3 beats.
4. Stop reading – 1 beat, listen – 3 beats.
5. Go to the window – 8 beats (1 to each step).
6. Rap on the window – 16 beats (1 to each rap).
7. Turn away from the window – 4 beats.

■ Repeat the exercise in a variety of tempos, from the very slow to the very fast. Analyse the different moods and feelings different tempos create.
■ Change the basic metre.
Instead of a basic metre of four plain beats, 4/4, where each beat can have 1,2,4,8,16 notes, we can have a metre of four dotted beats,12/8, where each beat can have 3,6,9,12 notes. The first metre is like walking, the second like skipping.
■ Do the scene in a dotted rhythm, in various tempos.
Analyse the different moods and feelings the change of metre produces.

INNER TEMPO-RHYTHM

Our feelings and thoughts also have a particular **Tempo-rhythm**, according to the situation we are in. We talk about our minds 'racing' when we are excited.

STUDIO EXERCISES
These exercises are designed to explore inner **Tempo-rhythm**. Imagine yourself in the following situations, using **Emotion Memory** if it helps:
■ It is a dark night. You are in an empty street. You hear footsteps approaching.
■ Spring. You are in the park. The birds are singing, the trees are in leaf, the flowers are blooming.
■ You hear the sound of passing cars. A group of young people arrives, talking, laughing, singing.
Did you feel in a different **Tempo-rhythm** in each case? Were there any physical effects? Did your pulse rate increase, decrease, did your rate of breathing alter?

THE INFLUENCE OF MENTAL STATES ON OUTER TEMPO-RHYTHM

Let us look further at the physical effect of mental states.
As a transitional exercise, re-do the Studio Exercise in the previous section, fixing your own tempo and retaining the

rhythmic pattern. Allow a mood to be created. Then improvise the rest of the scene after step 7 (Turn away from the window), allowing that mood to dictate the **Tempo-rhythm** of your actions. It may change, it may not, don't pre-empt your decision. Let it happen.

Analyse the results.

Studio Exercises

These exercises are based on activities performed in a particular mental state, or mood.

That state must arise from a situation or a precise set of circumstances which you will have to work out in as much detail as possible. The clearer your understanding of the situation, the clearer your feelings and thoughts will be, and the clearer your actions and your **Tempo-rhythm**.

If you encounter a block at any point, go back to the situation and fill out the details more clearly.

Each exercise is based on an **Organic Action**.

■ The basic **Organic Action** is getting dressed.
  Dress:
  • To go to lunch with someone you dislike but whom you need.
  • To go to work. You have plenty of time. You can take the bus or the Underground.
  • To meet your lover.
  • To go to a lawyer about an unexpected inheritance.
  • To go to the dentist to have a tooth out.
Let the situation determine the **Tempo-rhythm** in each case. The actions will be basically the same.

■ Using this as a model, create various situations round the following activities:
  • Looking for something you have lost.
  • Hiding.
  • Waiting.
  • Packing a suitcase.
  • Tidying your room.
  • Writing a letter.
  • Doing the washing-up.*

CONTRADICTORY INNER AND OUTER TEMPO-RHYTHMS

Sometimes we move in one **Tempo-rhythm** and feel in another.

There are occasions, for example, when we have to appear outwardly calm and in control although we are in turmoil on the inside.

STUDIO EXERCISES

■ You are being interviewed for entry into a theatre school or for a part you want to play. You are desperate for it. You are tense and nervous but you want to appear relaxed, friendly, not too pushy and not over-anxious to be cast.*

■ Someone is telling you a very long and very boring story and you are almost jumping with frustration but you remain outwardly polite.*

■ You are in a difficult situation and you realise that the only solution is a display of temper but, in order to remain in control, you must be calm inside and manipulate your own behaviour.*

VARYING TEMPO-RHYTHMS

Improvised Scenes with Many Characters and Many Tempo-rhythms

In a group scene, each character will have an individual **Tempo-rhythm**.

STUDIO EXERCISES

■ Create a scene in:
  • A supermarket.*
  • A railway/ bus station.
  • A self-service café.*

The group decides the time of day, circumstances etc. Everyone, as himself/herself, creates a situation that will determine, if possible, only one outer and one inner **Tempo-rhythm** (not necessarily identical) for the scene.

Individual Scenes with Varying Tempo-rhythms

There is a wide range of tempos, from the very slow to the very fast. Terms exist in music for most speeds – *lento, allegro, presto* – sometimes with metronome marks to indicate the exact speed. If you have a knowledge of music, use it to help you in this exercise.

EXERCISE
■ Select three contrasted tempos, inner and outer, and create a situation in which all three occur.

Group Scenes with Varying Tempo-rhythms

STUDIO EXERCISES
■ Go back to the group scenes, or invent something similar, and replay them this time with each character using three contrasting **Tempo-rhythms**, which must, of course, be justified.
■ Create a situation e.g. waiting for someone at an airport when the plane is early/delayed/cancelled and see how your changing mood dictates changes in **Tempo-rhythm**. How is your own **Tempo-rhythm** influenced, if at all, by interaction with other people?

Verbal Action

In these classes we shall look at the following aspects of language in terms of logical and expressive functions:

>   Punctuation
>   Pauses
>   Stress

Speech is action, no less than gesture and movement. Just as we study and analyse the nature of physical action, so we need to study and analyse the nature of verbal action.

The actual training of the vocal instrument is a matter for specialists. We need to go regularly to voice class.

There remains, however, the problem of how we respond to language, whether we understand the way it works and are able to find clues to feeling, attitudes, intentions from the way in which the words are arranged on the page. In modern criminal investigation, the police often derive crucial information about the person they are seeking through a forensic analysis of his vocal and speech patterns. We need to develop similar skills with the printed word.

We do not assume, if we are called on to perform a dance in the course of a play, that we can simply do it. We have to master the steps, the rhythm, control our body. We do not assume that because we can walk or run we can also dance in *Swan Lake* or *West Side Story*. We do not normally speak in blank verse (as in Shakespeare) or in rhymed couplets (as in Molière or Racine) and should not assume that mastering those forms will come easily simply because we speak every day.

Dialogue is not everyday speech, however much it may look like it. The plays of Noël Coward, Harold Pinter and David Mamet may seem to be composed of ordinary expressions but the dialogue is, in fact, tightly organised, like music. They could not be mistaken for each other, however 'everyday' the vocabulary. They sound and feel different. How are we to analyse and master differences like that?

Some major film, television and theatre companies employ regular voice consultants and dialogue coaches to guide actors through difficult moments, but such expert advice is not always available and we need to be able to work effectively on our own.

We are not linguists, but we can acquire a basic knowledge of language, of the way it works and how the way it is written down indicates the way it should be spoken.

PUNCTUATION

Punctuation has two functions. It divides a long statement up into units so that it can be more easily understood. That is its logical function. It can also indicate phrasing, breathing, the rise and fall of the voice, the musical pattern. That is its expressive function. In music, the phrasing is indicated by curved lines of varying lengths.

In both cases, as we are addressing someone else (even our own inner self), it is a way of controlling the listener's response.

The Comma

The comma indicates that I have not finished what I want to say. I will continue. Usually the voice rises slightly in pitch, so that the listener waits for the rest of the sentence and will continue to wait if a number of phrases end in a comma:

I don't want apples, or pears, or cucumbers.

The Full Stop

The full stop indicates that the statement is complete. The voice drops, indicating the end:

I don't want apples, or pears, or cucumbers, I want peaches.

The Question Mark

I want a response and the strength of my want is expressed by a marked rise in pitch at the end of the sentence. If I don't get an answer, I may repeat the question, rising higher at the end of the sentence every time:

Are you coming, or not?

A Row of Dots

This indicates that my thoughts have trailed away, I have lost track of what I was going to say:

I was trying to remember where I put my keys but I . . .

A Dash

This indicates an afterthought, or a comment on what has just been said:

He's very rich – and how!

The Exclamation Mark

This emphasises a command, a strong expression of feeling (as in swearing), or a statement that is made very emphatically, indicating that you expect it to be taken seriously:

Come here! All right then, **** off! Don't say I didn't warn you!

The Colon and Semicolon

Modern punctuation makes less and less use of these but they are found in earlier writing. Both indicate a kind of half-close, somewhere in pitch between the comma and the full stop.

PAUSES

Punctuation shows us on the page how a sentence is made up, what its constituent parts are; it guides the eye so that the meaning becomes clear and the information can be taken in effectively. The pause performs a similar function for the ear. It breaks up the sentence into manageable parts. A statement that

is driven through without pauses can be very difficult to follow
or can even become meaningless.

The simplest example of phrasing is what Stanislavski called
the 'Two-column sentence' which is divided into two by a
comma:

If you don't do as I say, I shall leave.

At the comma we mark a pause.

The first half of the sentence constitutes a warning, and the
voice rises, thus creating a sense of expectation. The pause
enables the listener to digest the information he has received.
The second half of the sentence indicates the consequences of
the warning. The voice drops to the full stop, suggesting finality.

This is what Stanislavski called the 'logical pause', since it is concerned with the argument grouping together words which belong
together, and separating different groups from one another.

There is, however, another kind of pause, the 'psychological
pause', which stems from inner impulse or the action and may
break up a text differently. The logical pause is dictated by the
content, the psychological pause indicates the state of mind of
the speaker and changes of mood.

In delivering a text, both kinds of pauses need to be combined.

The most obvious examples are verse texts, where the writing
is continuous and the metre urges the actor forward so as to
maintain the flow. We have to find ways, however, of expressing
intense inner feeling within the formal structure of the writing.

Stanislavski took the example of *King Lear* Act V, scene iii.
Lear, who has regained his sanity, carries in the dead body of
Cordelia. He alternates between frustrated anger and almost
uncontrollable grief.

Shakespeare's text is:

A plague upon you, murderous traitors all.
I might have saved her; now she's gone forever. –
Cordelia, Cordelia: stay a little. Ha?
What is't thou sayst? – Her voice was ever soft,
Gentle, and low, an excellent thing in women. –
I killed the slave that was a-hanging thee.

First establishing the logical pauses, Stanislavski found:

A plague upon you, murderous traitors all. [*logical pause*]
I might have saved her; [*logical pause*] now she's gone forever.
–

Cordelia, Cordelia: stay a little. Ha?
What is't thou sayst? – Her voice was ever soft,
Gentle, and low, an excellent thing in women. –
I killed the slave that was a-hanging thee.

Then, looking for the psychological pauses, he suggested:

A plague upon you, murderous traitors all.
I might have saved her; now she's gone forever. –
   [*psychological pause*]
Cordelia, Cordelia: stay a little. Ha?
What is't thou sayst? – [*psychological pause*] Her voice was ever
   soft,
Gentle, and low, an excellent thing in women. – [*psychological
   pause*]
I killed the slave that was a-hanging thee.

It is important to note here that the psychological pauses are actually indicated by the punctuation, wherever we find a full stop, or a question mark followed by dashes.

Psychological pauses must be used very cautiously. If there are too many, they replace the logical pause and the sense is lost. They must, therefore, be planned and, of course, justified. In the *Lear* passage, the psychological pauses coincide with changes of thought and focus, a switch in the **Object of Attention**.

If we combine logical pauses and psychological pauses we may find:

A plague upon you, murderous traitors all. [*logical pause*]
I might have saved her; [*logical pause*] now she's gone forever.
   – [*psychological pause*]
Cordelia, Cordelia: stay a little. Ha?
What is't thou sayst? – [*psychological pause*] Her voice was ever
   soft,

Gentle, and low, an excellent thing in women. – [*psychological pause*]

I killed the slave that was a-hanging thee.

A pause should not be a gap. It must be an integral part of the dialogue. Dialogue at every point has its own **Tempo-rhythm** and the pauses must be measured within that **Tempo-rhythm**.

STRESS

Stress adds vitality to speech by denoting personal involvement in what is being said. It also ensures greater precision of meaning.

Take the simple sentence:

I walked here.

We can stress this in three ways, each with a different meaning:

I walked here (others didn't).

I *walked* here (I didn't drive).

I walked *here* (not somewhere else).

Stress can not only merely change meaning, but also reveal attitude, feeling.

Let us take the sentence:

All I want is for you to get out of here and leave me alone.

This will be differently stressed according to the state of mind of the speaker.

Angry:

All I want is for you to get out of here and leave me *alone*.

Attempting self-control:

All I want is for *you* to get out of here and leave me *alone*.

Weary:

All I want is for you to get out of here and leave me alone.

In each case, the depth, force and length of the stress will note the degree of emotion.

In any given phrase, or group of words, there is a keyword, what Stanislavski called a 'magnet', around which the other words cluster. A statement, made up of individual phrases, would contain a limited number of keywords, which are stressed. This Stanislavski called the *logical stress.*

Having too many stresses in a statement, like having too many pauses, obscures the meaning, makes the sentence more difficult to follow. If everything is important, then nothing is important.

Stanislavski distinguished three levels of logical stress in descending order of strength:

Level 1: major stress, falls on the word(s) in the main clause.
Level 2: medium stress, falls on the words in dependent clauses.
Level 3: minor stress, occurs in parentheses.

Stanislavski took a sentence from Gogol's *Taras Bulba:*

'Where's the old woman?' – that is what he usually called his
wife – 'Look alive, old woman, prepare us food, the way
we have to go is great.'

A major stress falls on the first 'old woman' and later 'food'. A medium stress falls on 'way' and a minor stress on 'wife' in the parenthesis.

In addition to the logical stress, there is what Stanislavski called the 'symbolic' or 'artistic' stress.

The artistic stress paints a more vivid picture in the imagination of the listener.

Stanislavski took the sentence:

'A block and in it an axe, that is what he saw before him.'

The logical stress, as in straight reporting, gives:

'A block and in it an axe, *that* is what he saw before him.'

The artistic stress:

'A *block* and in it an *axe*, that he what he saw before him.'

This focuses the listener's imagination on the picture in the speaker's mind. A minor stress will occur on 'that'.

EXERCISES

■ Take extracts from daily papers and magazines, analyse them
for punctuation, pause and stress, and read them out loud to
convey information clearly. Do this on a daily basis.

■ Go back to the extract from *Macbeth* (pp. *67–68)* and see how
the tension, the inner turmoil is indicated by the way in which
the lines are broken up between the two characters, the
jerkiness of the rhythms, which suggest fear, wariness,
breathlessness. Find other passages from plays or literature,
where the shape of the emotion is suggested by the layout of
the sentences.

Physical Characterisation

As actors and human beings, we can only have our own thoughts and feelings, we can't exchange them for somebody else's. But we can change bodies. We can walk differently, talk differently, put on padding, wigs, make-up, disguise ourselves so that even our best friends won't know us.

This capacity to hide ourselves offers a kind of protection and security that actors, in varying degrees, need. There are aspects of our personality which we often do not like, often do not approve of, and which we would rather other people didn't know about. But we may need precisely those aspects for a character.

If, for a time, we don't look like ourselves but like someone else, we can make use of those hidden aspects of our personality in safety, we have a mask to hide behind.

We need to explore the effect of physical form and appearance on the way we feel and behave.

Like everything else in our work, physical characterisation must be precise, exact and founded in reality.

Let us start with three exploratory examples of the effect of physical differences on behaviour:

STUDIO EXERCISES
- Blindfold yourself and be led around.
- Stop your ears so you can't hear anything and try to communicate.
- Strap your writing hand behind your back and try to perform simple physical tasks.

Now let us look at three broad categories of physical characterisation:

> Natural.
> Professional.
> Social.

STUDIO EXERCISES

Natural

■ Observe and copy, if you can, the external characteristics of:
  • Old people – how they walk, sit, rise etc.
  • Fat people.
  • People with a limp.
  • People who are drunk.
  • People with some kind of disability.
  • People who are very tall.
  • People who are very short.

Professional

■ Observe and copy the characteristics of:
  • Boxers.
  • Professional soldiers.
  • Weightlifters.
  • Ballet dancers.
  • Office or sedentary workers.
  • Fashion models.*

What effect has professional training/habit had on the way their bodies perform?

Social

■ Observe people in:
  • The street.
  • A department store.
  • A train.
  • A restaurant.

Look at their clothes, their make-up, their gestures, their table manners. Listen to their speech, their vocabulary. Does all this information add up to a coherent picture? If so, of what? Could you tell which class, profession etc. they belong to? How well-off they are? Are there social conventions which demand that certain groups of people dress and behave in a certain way? Are there contradictions? What about a well-spoken beggar?

JUSTIFICATION

The work so far has been a kind of laboratory study. But just as words can be inflected, have different weight, length, colour in different circumstances, so physical statements can be inflected by being made in specific contexts, in real situations. As elsewhere in our work, the basic actions, the physical elements may be constant but it is only a fully thought-out situation which brings them alive and makes them human. Not all disabled people, for example, have the same attitude towards their disability. Not all exceptionally gifted people view their gifts in the same way. Merely copying someone's external characteristics is not acting. The characteristics must have a reason, a basis in the total life of the person, they must be justified. Richard III and Quasimodo were both hunchbacks, but they were very different hunchbacks.

Studio Exercises

■ You have a broken arm. Justify it. How and where did it get broken? Were you responsible or not? How have you reacted to it? How have other people reacted to it, particularly, say, if it was your fault?

■ Model your appearance on someone you have seen and observed. Justify it. Imagine how they live, what their past is, what their profession is, what they are likely to believe in, how they will vote etc.*

■ Take a character you know well from a modern play and whom you would like to play. Create his/her appearance and justify it from the information given in the script. See how far the externals help you understand the character's behaviour and the dialogue.*

Total Action

In these classes we shall look at:

> The supertask
> Through-action
> Counter-through-action

Having studied all the aspects of our technique we now have to bring them together in the service of the play, otherwise they remain unrelated skills with no purpose. At the root of a play is a theme, or subject, what the play is *about*, the reason it was written, the goal to which all the individual tasks which the actors perform are directed. This is the **Supertask**. All the actions we perform should be logical and coherent, they should create the **Through-action**. For each **Through-action** there is an opposing **Counter-through-action**, when someone else's wants, tasks run counter to our own. One of our problems is to decide what, in terms of the overall meaning of the play, are the **Supertask**, the **Through-action** and the **Counter-through-action**.

Generally, when the actions run counter to the purpose of the central character(s) they are called the **Counter-through-action**. For example, the 'hero' will have the **Through-action,** the 'villain' the **Counter-through-action**.

SUPERTASK: HISTORICAL EXAMPLES

Take two legendary, historical figures, King Arthur and Joan of Arc.

If we look at the story of Arthur and the Knights of the Round Table, what is the theme, the subject, the **Supertask**?
The establishment of order and justice.

The **Through-action** of Arthur, Merlin and his knights is to achieve that end.

The **Counter-through-action** of Mordred and Morgana is to defeat Arthur's purpose.

If, similarly, we look at the story of Joan of Arc, what is the **Supertask**?

The liberation of France from the English.

The **Through-action** of Joan and her allies is to wage a victorious war and establish Charles VII as sole King of France.

The **Counter-through-action** of the English and the Duke of Burgundy is to defeat her and keep the King of France weak.

SUPERTASK: DRAMATIC EXAMPLES

In the case of a play, to verify a **Supertask** we need to make sure it is valid for every major **Episode.**

Let us turn to Chekhov's *Three Sisters* as an example.

STUDIO NOTES

*Stanislavski suggested that the **Supertask** for the play was:*

The desire for fulfilment, to live a full life.

He outlined the first three acts as follows:

In Act One, a year of mourning has passed, spring has come. Life begins again. It is Irina's birthday and there is a noisy, happy lunch party to which officers from the local garrison have been invited. Andrei has found a wife.

In Act Two, love flourishes, there is the noise of happy young people.

In Act Three, the need for a new, a better life, the longing for a way out of the rut is reaffirmed.

If we follow this analysis through, we find that in Act Four, despite the collapse of everyone's hopes, and the tragedy, Olga affirms the possibility of a better life in the future.

If, having accepted this definition of the **Supertask**, we look at the play in terms of **Through-action** and **Counter-through-action**:

The Prozorov family (Olga, Masha, Irina, Andrei), Vershinin and Tusenbach all seek happiness. That is their **Through-action.**

Their family and friends, wittingly or unwittingly, frustrate their desires. That is their **Counter-through-action**.

The definition of the **Supertask** colours the whole approach to the play, since it is the yardstick by which we judge all our other decisions. However, it is not always easy to find the right definition. We have to regard our first definition as provisional, to be tested out as we work more closely on the play.

Let us take Chekhov's last play, *The Cherry Orchard*. We might decide that the **Supertask** is:

The need to adapt to changing times.

We can justify this:

Act One. Ranevskaya returns home to Russia from Paris, abandoning her worthless lover, to find the mortgage on her estate cannot be paid, unless she sells her cherry orchard. Her neighbour, Lopakhin, suggests a profitable scheme to build summer villas for holiday-makers.

Act Two. The dominant theme is failure, admissions of personal failure, and a recognition of national failure. Ranevskaya cannot bring herself to accept Lopakhin's scheme because it is 'vulgar'.

Act Three. The cherry orchard is sold. Ranevskaya loses everything.

Act Four. The family abandons their home and is scattered. The cherry orchard is chopped down.

If we accept this **Supertask**, then the **Through-action** is represented by Lopakhin, who urges Ranevskaya to face facts and sell. Ranevskaya, by resisting his advice, represents the **Counter-through-action**.

But what if we define a different **Supertask**?

The need to resist change, preserve traditional values, and fight against vulgar commercialism.

If this is the **Supertask**, then Ranevskaya represents the principal **Through-action** and Lopakhin the principal **Counter-through-action**.

How can we decide between the two?

We need to examine another character, Trofimov, who represents the younger generation of intellectuals. His constant theme is Russia ('All Russia is our orchard'), its past and its future. He talks of transforming society. At the end of the play, Trofimov, the idealist, who refuses material values, states his approval of Lopakhin and his positive actions.

Perhaps, then, we should opt for the notion of response to change and reject our second definition? We can only make a definite decision during the process of rehearsal. We start with a working definition of the **Supertask** and judge our immediate actions against it. But close exploration of the events in the play as movement, words and thoughts in space, rather than as print on a page, may lead us to revise our working definition in the light of what we have discovered we actually need to do. This two-way traffic, this cross-verification of the general and the local is essential if we are to create a performance which has a unity of purpose and a coherence which the audience can perceive.

Performance Mode

We have studied all the elements of the 'system'. Our instrument is tuned and is now ready to respond to the spontaneous reactions that spring from our subconscious. We are ready for creative, rehearsal work, and to use the Method of Physical Action. We are in **Performance Mode**. And because we are technically aware, we are able to scrutinise, evaluate and shape our discoveries into a coherent performance, a play.

PART THREE

The Method of Physical Action in Rehearsal

Students at the Studio began to work on plays towards the end of the second year.

The object of the rehearsal classes was to establish a method of work that would apply to plays of all kinds, both contemporary and classic. The plays which the students worked on included texts by Ostrovski and Shakespeare. The function of the directors and indeed of Stanislavski himself at the Studio during the third year was to guide students towards creating a role through analysis, questioning, challenge and encouragement.

Stanislavski conceived an ideal company that would be composed entirely of actors who were technical masters, who could approach a text methodically and creatively, and ask all the right questions and find appropriate answers. The staging would then emerge organically and naturally. Actors should not speak or move just because 'that's what the director told me to do'. ·

In the Method of Physical Action, rehearsal is not a process of drilling pre-existing ideas which may be no more than superficial. It is a process of discovery, experiment, trying out, the discovery and revelation of meaning through careful analysis and experiment.

At the Studio, there was no attempt to reach a final, polished performance until the fourth year. Stanislavski died, however, before the fourth year of work began and therefore did not see students through the final stage of planning the production as an artistic whole. This was left to his assistants. We have a record of his work using the Method of Physical Action with trained professional actors in the last few months of his life, in the description by Vasili Toporkov of Stanislavski's work on *Tartuffe* in *Stanislavski in Rehearsal*.†

THE MODEL REHEARSAL METHOD

Stanislavski did not write down a definitive version of the Method of Physical Action. Indeed, he would have thought the whole idea of a definitive version absurd. The Method of Physical Action evolved over a period of just over twenty years from 1916 until 1938.

We can, however, construct a model of his method using drafts, his own notebooks and the outline he gave to his assistants at the Studio.‡

The same fundamental principles underlie all his statements:

1. That the basis for every role and for the performance as a whole is a detailed understanding of the action of the play, the dramatic situation, the **Given Circumstances**, the historical and social background.
2. That the actors must work on the basis of their own resources and life experiences, creating the **Necessity** of their actions out of their study and experiment.
3. That the author's text must be respected, studied and served.
4. That all the individual contributions and creative efforts must be shaped into a coherent, artistic whole, an ensemble performance.

Work on a play, in Stanislavski's view, takes at least a year and moves in distinct phases:

Actors have to work:

> Individually, using all the techniques of the 'system' to create a role.
> Collectively, as an ensemble, sharing their discoveries, to create a play.

† Trans. Christine Edwards (Theatre Arts Books, New York, 1979).

‡ In chronological order these are: *Gore ot Uma (1916–20)*, in *Sobranie Sochinenij v devjati tomakh*, t. 4, pp. 48–173; *Otello (1930–33)* in *SS* t. 4, pp. 276–323; Novitskaya, op. cit., pp. 209-12; *Podkhod k Rolju (1936–7)*, in *SS* t. 4, pp. 377–79.

Because of the length of the rehearsal period and the need to collaborate with other actors, Stanislavski insisted that his students keep notebooks, write down their findings, so that they could:

> be clear about their intentions, which had to be shared with others
>
> they could always refer back to what they had done.

Writing down is a way of making sure that I really know, don't just think I know, what I am doing. I don't have to write an essay, or a report, I just have to note down what is essential so that, in rehearsal, I can communicate it to others, as part of a continuous creative process.

Preliminary: First Impressions

The first time you, as an actor, read a play is, perhaps, the most crucial moment in the creative process. It is the first and perhaps the last time you will experience it as an audience. This is not a critical or analytical reading. Read it with an open mind and be as receptive as possible to what it has to offer. These first impressions often provide the motivation to create, they are seeds that are planted in the mind that will grow. Read the play several times, soak it up, learn what happens. At the end you should be able to summarise the action even of a complex play in ten minutes. Members of the group can compare their accounts.

Phase One: Analysis Through Action

Analysis proceeds in stages of ever increasing detail and complexity:

- ■ Improvise basic elements in the story. What are the **Given Circumstances** at any particular moment? How do you respond to them? Ask yourself, 'What would I do, here, today, now, if I were in these, or similar circumstances?' Fill in the gaps, what has happened between entrances, the scene the dramatist hasn't included, the **Before-time**. Work right through the play.

■ Summarise the action of the play once again, but in greater detail, explore the **Given Circumstances** more deeply, find more precise physical actions to meet the situations.

■ On the basis of work so far, define a provisional **Supertask**.

■ Define where the characters are going. What is their goal? What it is they want? What is the overall purpose of what they do? What is their **Through-action**?

Breaking Down the Play

■ First divide the play into **Episodes**, the fewer the better, so that the action of the play is still clear and not lost in a welter of detail.

■ Each actor has to find the **Basic Action** in the **Episode**, still working on the basis of 'what would I do, here, today now, if . . .'

■ Divide the **Episodes** into **Facts** or **Events**. Each actor has to find the **Task** for his character and the logical sequence of actions necessary to fulfil it. Write down the sequence of **Tasks** and the **Actions** they require.

[Note: This is most easily done in columns, a practice Stanislavski adopted early on. Write down the **Task** in one column and the **Actions** in the second. This not only helps you make clear decisions, it also helps you verify whether the sequence of actions is really logical and matches the logical sequence of the **Tasks**.]

■ Discuss, as a group, your **Tasks** and **Actions**.

■ Improvise the **Facts/Events** several times, gradually stripping what you do down to essentials. Still work on the basis of 'What would I do, here, today, now, if . . .?' Allow the logic, the physical truth of what you are doing to create a state of belief in the action of the play and in your own actions.

■ Define the pace, the speed, the **Tempo-rhythm** of each physical action and of the **Fact/Event** as a whole. The **Tempo-rhythm** is related to the nature of the **Task**, the intention, the urgency or not of the situation.

■ Begin to establish the matching sequence of thoughts and images that lies behind the **Tasks** and **Actions**, and justifies them – the **Subtext**.

Phase One leads to the **'I am Being'** and brings our subconscious mechanisms into play.

Phase Two: Transition to the Text

■ Read the play, as a group for the first time, bearing in mind the work that has been done using your own words in improvisation. Pay special attention to any lines that strike you, or make a strong impression. Note them down. Work through the play again, incorporating the words you have noted in your improvisations.

■ Read the play through several times, with each actor taking more detailed notes of the text each time. Examine the style of the writing, look up the meaning of difficult words or phrases. Make a list of historical and social topics that need to be investigated to understand the background of the play. Improvise each time through, using more and more of the written dialogue where and when it seems natural.

■ Consciously study the dialogue. The actors learn their lines. For the moment they keep them in their head. They don't speak them out loud. They must not become so used to them they that start to be mechanical. There is still much more to discover.

■ Work through the play again, probing deeper into the **Given circumstances**, justifying your actions in greater detail. Keep the dialogue in your head, replace it with 'la la la' or other sounds.

■ The play is 'performed' sitting round the table, without action and without gesture, 'sitting on one's hands'. **Episode** by **Episode**, **Fact** by **Fact**, each actor says his/her lines and at the same time explains the thoughts and intentions, the **Subtext** he/she has noted down, to the other actors.

■ Repeat the process, this time using hands and small body movements, still sitting round the table.

■ Repeat the process on stage, using improvised moves.

■ The actors work more consciously on external characterisation. What does the person whose thoughts, ideas and behaviour patterns they have defined look like? The process of improvisation and information in the text will have laid the foundations of the physical appearance, which will begin to emerge naturally, organically. However, the actors should experiment with physical ideas – a walk, a characteristic gesture – that will round out the external characterisation. Physical awareness of the character may also affect the inner characterisation and bring about changes in the **Subtext** and behaviour patterns.

Phase Three: Planning the Production

- Work through the play, establishing and fixing the moves, the pattern of staging which has either been agreed upon by the group as a whole, or suggested by the director on the basis of the group's work.
- Work through the play, using only the agreed moves and the author's dialogue, keeping the **Subtext** in your heads. Begin to establish the plan for the whole, the **Perspective**, finding the right level, the right **Tempo-rhythm** for each scene in relation to all the others. The climaxes, the key moments, must emerge more clearly, more forcefully than the others. The actor has a double function here: first, as an artist who plots the course of his role – the climaxes and moments of relaxation, the moments of high and low energy – and sees his role within the context of the dramatic structure as a whole; second, as an actor who can only play a succession of **Tasks**, **Here, Today, Now**, a series of 'now' moments. The level for each 'now' moment is determined at this stage so that, in actual performance, the actor can forget the plan.
- Check that the **Through-action**, or **Counter-through-action** is clear in each case, for every actor.
- Check that the **Supertask** defined in the early stages of rehearsal is the right one. Redefine if necessary.

PRACTICAL EXAMPLES OF THE METHOD OF PHYSICAL ACTION

Let us look at some examples of the way in which the Method

of Physical Action has or can be used in the various phases.

Example One: *The Cherry Orchard*

Phase One

Let us start at the beginning of the process, after the actors have read the play on their own several times, are familiar with it and begin to analyse the action.

If we divide the play first into broad **Episodes**, we see that each act roughly constitutes an **Episode**.

Episode 1. Ranevskaya returns home to her estate in Russia from Paris.

Episode 2. The last family outing.

Episode 3. The cherry orchard is sold.

Episode 4. Ranevskaya and her family leave their home for ever.

We can then break down the **Episodes** into **Facts/Events**.

Example: **Episode 1.**
Facts:

1. Lopakhin and the maid, Dunyasha, are waiting at the house for Ranevskaya to arrive. The train is two hours late.
2. The other members of the family, Gaev, Varya and friends are at the station waiting.
3. Epikhodov arrives with flowers for Dunyasha whom he wishes to marry.
4. Ranevskaya and company arrive at the house and go into the nursery.
5. Ranevskaya's life of poverty in France is revealed. The possible sale of the cherry orchard in announced.
6. Lopakhin suggests a way out of their financial difficulties by building summer villas.
7. Trofimov, once tutor to Ranevskaya's son who was killed in an accident, arrives to pay his respects.

8. Gaev promises to go to Varya's great-aunt to ask for financial help.
9. Anya falls asleep as Varya talks. Varya takes her to bed.
10. Trofimov, left alone, reveals his love for Anya.

■ The **Before-time** for each character has to be established through improvisation.
At the house: Lopakhin, Dunyasha, Epikhodov.
At the station: Varya (refer back to Lilina's plan in Part Two, pp. 51–52), Gaev, Ranevskaya, Anya, Yasha.
■ Finally, we must establish the provisional **Supertask**.
What is the play about? How do we provisionally define the
Supertask?
Responding to changing times and a new Russia.

The same approach can be applied to much more complex plays.

Example Two: *Romeo and Juliet*

Phase One
After Stanislavski's death in 1938, the members of the Studio continued to work on *Romeo and Juliet*. They broke the play down into **Episodes** and **Facts**.

STUDIO NOTES†
*We divided the whole play into **Episodes**, act by act.‡ The result was as follows:*

First Act

1. *Don't fear life but death. The vendetta between two opposing houses.*
2. *Romeo's secret revealed: he is in love with Rosalind.*
3. *Juliet mother informs her of a change in her life – she is betrothed to Paris.*
4. *Despite their forebodings and doubts, Romeo and his friends go to the Capulet ball.*

† Novitskaya, op. cit., pp. 212–14.
‡ The **Episodes** do not correspond to the normal act divisions, which divisions were not, in fact, Shakespeare's but introduced later by printers and editors.

5. *Romeo and Juliet meet – love at first sight.*

Second Act

1. *Romeo is rescued from an ambush.*
2. *Romeo and Juliet meet in the garden – all obstacles are overcome.*
3. *Romeo persuades Friar Lawrence to perform a secret marriage.*
4. *Despite the difficulties his friends raise, Romeo discusses his future plans with the Nurse.*
5. *Juliet learns the joyful news from the Nurse of her secret marriage to Romeo.*
6. *The secret wedding.*

Third Act

1. *Fresh obstacles in the path of love. Incensed by the death of Mercutio, Romeo kills Tybalt.*
2. *Juliet's love is so great that she justifies Romeo's action – love overcomes grief.*
3. *Romeo protests against his banishment; exile, life without Juliet is worse than death.*
4. *With great difficulty Friar Lawrence and the Nurse persuade Romeo to yield to the Duke's will.*
5. *The secret parting of Romeo and Juliet for a long time.*
6. *Juliet is at war with her family (she categorically refuses to marry Paris).*

Fourth Act

1. *Friar Lawrence finds a way to rescue Juliet from her marriage to Paris.*
2. *Juliet makes a show of obeying her parents (fictitious submission to her parents).*
3. *Juliet drinks the sleeping potion.*
4. *The Capulets prepare for the wedding.*
5. *The Capulets are overcome by inconsolable grief – the 'death' of Juliet.*
6. *The news of Juliet's death makes Romeo decide to die.*
7. *Romeo brushes aside all obstacles and goes to Juliet's tomb (mortal combat between Romeo and Paris).*
8. *Romeo and Juliet cannot, won't part – better to die together.*
9. *Love conquers death. Reconciliation of the two rival houses.*

*Each **Episode** was then broken down into **Facts**.*
Example: Act IV. Episode 1. Friar Lawrence finds a way to rescue Juliet from her marriage to Paris.

Facts:

1. The Friar tries to find a way to persuade Paris to refuse the marriage or not to rush ahead with it.
2. The unexpected meeting between Juliet and Paris in the Friar's cell.
3. Juliet politely takes leave of Paris.
4. Juliet implores the Friar to save her from a second marriage.
5. Juliet resolutely grasps at the desperate and dangerous solution the Friar offers.
6. The Friar explains his plan of action.
7. Juliet leaves.

*The **Basic Action** for each character in this **Episode** is:*
Paris: To fix the marriage as soon as possible.
Friar: To help Juliet or find a way to avoid a detestable second marriage.
Juliet: To find a way to help, to save my love.

Example Three: *Romeo and Juliet*

Phase One

As an exercise in filling in the gaps left by Shakespeare, the group improvised a scene immediately following Act IV, Episode 1, in which Juliet submits to her father.

The results of the exercise, from Juliet's point of view, were set out, in accordance with the practice of the Studio, in four columns, as shown in the table on the opposite page:

1. The brief text they had written.
2. Juliet's outer action, the meeting between father and daughter.
3. Juliet's **Subtext**, the **Inner Monologue** behind the outer dialogue.
4. Juliet's inner action, making sure she carries out the Friar's plan effectively.

Improvised Text	Outer Action	Subtext	Inner Action
	I enter, putting on 'a good face'.	Prepare to be married. Dear God!	I weigh up the situation. I keep my self-control.
CAPULET			
So, you obstinate child, where have you been idling your time away?	I try to maintain that appearance.		I reproach, blame my father.
JULIET			
To good Father Lawrence, to repent my resistance to your will. He bade me fall humbly on my knees and ask forgiveness.	I am penitent.	Idling my time? Not at all, I've just been to see a friend, my only friend. Repent indeed! The Friar has offered me help!	I thank the monk who will make everything come right. I allay my father's suspicions.
Pardon me, I beg you!	I Adopt a humble attitude.	I must do what the Friar told me. That's	I put my father in the right frame of mind,
I submit to your will.		not hard but I mustn't	finally lull his vigilance.
	I look imploring. I agree to the marriage, showing total submission.	give myself away! But that will never happen!	I do what the Friar told me as quickly as possible. (Quick exit)†

† Novitskaja, op. cit., p. 215.

Example Four: *Late Love*
Phase Two

Let us now take the moment in Phase Two when the actors are working fully with the written dialogue but are exchanging their **Subtext** as well as their lines.

At the Studio, a group of students worked on Ostrovski's *Late Love*. They left a record of their detailed work on the opening of the play.

■ Given Circumstances.

The heroine, Lyudmila, a woman now past her youth, has fallen in love with a much younger man, Nikolai, a lawyer. She lives with her father, also a lawyer, in a house owned by Shablova, Nikolai's mother. She hopes that she can somehow win his love, or, if not, his friendship.

■ Before-time

Shablova dotes on her son but is worried by his laziness, his
failure to earn a living, his spendthrift ways and the fact that he
stays away for days on end, vying with men richer than himself
for the favours of an older woman. Lyudmila and Shablova are
waiting for Nikolai to come home. It is late at night and the
weather is bad.

Episode 1: Waiting for Nikolai's return.

Fact 1: Both Lyudmila and Shablova think they have heard
Nikolai come back to the house.
Tasks:
> Lyudmila: I want secretly to make sure Nikolai is home safe.
> Shablova: I want to see if he really has come home.

Fact 2: Shablova is suspicious.
Tasks:
> Lyudmila: I want to conceal my true motives.
> Shablova: I want to know if she is waiting for Nikolai.

Ostrovski's script is as follows.
  ACT ONE, SCENE ONE
  LYUDMILA *comes out of her room, listens, goes to the window.*
    SHABLOVA *comes from her room.*
  SHABLOVA (*Not seeing* LYUDMILA) I could have sworn I heard
    the garden gate. But I was mistaken. But I had my ears
    open. What weather. He's only got a light coat on . . .
    Where's my darling son got to? Oh, children, children –
    they break a mother's heart. Even my wandering tomcat
    won't stay out. He's here.
  LYUDMILA He's here? Is he really?
  SHABLOVA Oh, Lyudmila, I didn't see you there, I'm just
    standing here imagining things.
  LYUDMILA Did you say he's here?
  SHABLOVA Are you waiting for someone?
  LYUDMILA Me? Not at all. Only I heard you say he's here.
  SHABLOVA I was just thinking aloud. My head's in such a
    whirl, you see.

The two actresses went through the scene, using the written dialogue and the notes they had prepared setting out their **Tasks** and their own **Inner Monologue**, actions and thoughts. These were set out as usual in columns:

1. Inner, mental actions and decisions (**Tasks**) which remain unspoken.
2. The **Inner Monologue**, actions, author's ideas (such as stage directions) which are spoken out loud and communicated to the other actress.

The results of the talk-through can be set out in the table on the next page.†

At this stage, both actresses' **Inner Monologues** and inner action are set side by side in parallel columns so that the action and interaction is clear. Ostrovski's dialogue is in italics.

This scene illustrates the complexity of mental activity under an apparently simple exchange of words.

Example Five: *Hamlet*

A group of students at the Studio spent a year working on *Hamlet*. Stanislavski supervised the work through a series of masterclasses as detailed in Part Four. [23]

Before looking at Stanislavski's work, let us go through the exercise ourselves, using the Method of Physical Action at the end of Phase Two, when we are working only with Shakespeare's text.

PHASE ONE
■ Broad Summary of the Action

The story is Hamlet's. The play moves in very large blocks:

Hamlet is told by his father's ghost that he has been murdered by Claudius.

He tries to find out if the story is true.

He learns it is true but his uncle outsmarts him and sends him into exile to be murdered.

† Novitskaya, pp. 374–6.

LYUDMILA Inner Action Unspoken	Inner Monologue, action, author's ideas (such as stage directions) spoken aloud and communicated to the other actor	SHABLOVA Inner Monologue, action, author's ideas (such as stage directions) spoken aloud and communicated to the other actor	Inner Action Unspoken
Fact 1.			
	Lyudmila comes out of her room (stage direction).		
I listen.	– The gate banged.		
I question.	– Is that him?		
I wonder.	– He hasn't come. Is he still		
I decide to go to the window.	outside?		
I try to see.	– I'll have a look!	Comes out of her room, doesn't see	
	– No, can't see him. It's dark.	Lyudmila (stage direction).	
	Could anyone see anything?	– I think he's come	I prepare to
I try to understand.	– Where on earth has he been all this time? It's very late.		meet my son.
		I listen to make sure.	
I find a reason.		*I could have sworn I heard the garden gate.*	
	– Perhaps he's been detained on	I reject the idea.	
I listen attentively.	business?	*But I was mistaken.*	
I look out of the window.	– Who's that?	I laugh at myself.	
I reject the idea.		*Though I had my ears wide open.*	
I try to imagine.	– It was a tree!		
	– But where can he be?	I feel sorry for him.	
I try to calm down.		*What weather!*	
	– He's with a client, of course.	*He's only got a light coat on . . .*	
		Where's my darling son got to?	
		Oh, children, children – they break a mother's heart.	
		I reproach my son.	
I interpret what she's said.		*Even my wandering tomcat won't stay out.*	
		He's here.	
	– So it seems he's here.		
	I seize on what I've heard.	–Who's that?	
	– *He's here. Is he really?*	– Eh?	
Fact 2.		I am aware of someone else.	I confirm.
		– Yes, that's what I said.	
		She is obviously waiting for someone, I want to confirm my suspicions.	
		Are you waiting for someone?	
I interpret her tone.	She's noticed.	– who is it then?	I watch closely.
	I try to find a way out.		I have my doubts,
	Me?		I try to confirm
	I explain (conceal the truth).		my suspicions. I
	Nobody. Only I heard you say he's here.	– Nobody? A likely tale! She's	decide to sound
		waiting for Nikolai.	her out.
I get a grip on myself.	– So, he's not here! That's that!	Now I sound her out.	
		I explain my behaviour.	
		I was lost in my own thoughts.	
		I look for sympathy.	
		My head's in such a whirl, you see.	

He escapes and returns and finally takes revenge on his Claudius.

The **Episodes**
1. The ghost of Hamlet's father appears on the battlements.
2. Claudius establishes himself as the new king.
3. Hamlet is told about the ghost and agrees to watch that night.
4. Polonius' home. Ophelia is warned not to trust Hamlet's love and Laertes leaves for France.
5. Hamlet meets his father's ghost and learns of his murder.
6. Hamlet's 'madness'.
7. The performance of the play and its consequences.
8. Ophelia's madness and Laertes' return.
9. Hamlet's letter announcing his escape and return.
10. Claudius' plot with Laertes and the news of Ophelia's death.
12. The graveyard and Ophelia's funeral.
13. The duel and final retribution.
14. Fortinbras becomes king.

The **Before-time**
Claudius has murdered the king, his brother and Hamlet's father. He has married his sister-in-law, Gertrude, and occupied the throne. Hamlet, who was a student at the University of Wittenberg, has returned to the court. He is in love with Ophelia, the daughter of the king's chief minister, Polonius.

Provisional **Supertask**: *Just Retribution*
Hamlet's father has been murdered and his throne usurped by his brother. Hamlet himself has been denied rightful succession to the throne. Hamlet has been called upon to avenge his father's death but it must be the right kind of revenge. Claudius must not only die, he must also die in the right circumstances. Hamlet's father died, according to the theology which Hamlet accepts, in a state of sin and therefore has to spend a period of torment in Purgatory. Claudius must die similarly. When

Hamlet is presented with a golden opportunity to kill his uncle, Claudius is at prayer, and therefore in a state of grace, and if he dies, goes straight to heaven. Hence the search for just retribution, not mere retribution.

Through-action and Counter-through-action
Hamlet's **Through-action** is to achieve just retribution against his uncle.
Claudius's **Counter-through-action** is to do everything to hold on to his position.
All the other characters are drawn into one or the other.
Hamlet is aided by Horatio, the soldiers and the players.
Claudius is aided, wittingly or unwittingly, by the members of the court (Polonius, Laertes, Ophelia, Gertrude, Rosencrantz and Guildenstern).

Fact/Events
For example:
Episode 1 consists of the following **Facts**:

1. The guard changes.
2. Marcellus and Bernardo tell Horatio of the ghost.
3. Horatio is sceptical.
4. The ghost appears but refuses to speak.
5. Horatio recognises the ghost as Hamlet's father.
6. The ghost appears again.
7. The three decide to inform Hamlet of what they have seen.

PHASE ONE
Investigate this scene through:
1. Free improvisation of the dramatic situation: What would I do if **Here, Today, Now** I were to see a ghost? Using the six Ws:

Whence:	Where have I just come from?
Where:	Where am I?
When:	When is this happening?
What:	What am I doing?

Why: Why am I doing it?
Whither: Where am I going to now?

2. Exercises in **Emotion Memory**: cold, damp, snow, night, darkness, fear of the dark etc.

Work through the whole play in this manner a number of times, and in greater depth each time, define the **Given Circumstances** more and more precisely until they are clear and precise and the cast believe in them.

- Create the **Inner Monologues** and **Subtext**.
- Establish the **Tempo-rhythm** for all **Actions** and **Facts**.

PHASE TWO

- Read through the script several times. Note keywords and phrases in the written dialogue and use them in improvisation.
- Investigate topics which need to be researched. These include:
    1. What were considered to be the political duties of a king, or prince in Shakespeare's time? What were his essential qualities?
    2. What were the religious beliefs? What was Purgatory? What was understood by a 'state of grace'? What was the definition of incest?
    3. What were the views on power politics? Under what circumstances was it ever right to remove or assassinate a ruler?
    4. What was the sexual morality, the views of sex outside marriage?
    5. What were the social hierarchies? What were the distinctions of rank? How did this affect marriage?

TRANSITION TO THE TEXT

This is the difficult moment of transition when we no longer use improvised dialogue but Shakespeare's text. We cannot speak words which we do not fully understand. We have to explore them as fully as we have the **Tasks**, **Actions** and **Subtext**. The next crucial step is to examine the nature of the text, how it is formally structured, phrased, what its rhythms are.

When we have completed this work we will have established:

The **Before-time**.
The **Episodes**.
Our **Basic Actions**.
The **Fact/Events**.
The inner line of mental actions, what are our intentions, purposes, **Tasks**.
How we see events from our own point of view, what we think, which may not be what we say, the **Subtext**.
The results of our background research.

Let us now look at a specific example, and take a short but difficult **Fact** from **Episode 6**: Hamlet's 'madness'. This **Episode**, which is crucial to the development of the play, is textually the most difficult. This gives us an opportunity to look more closely at the relationship between text and **Subtext**.

If we are not to get lost in the detail, we need to hold on fast to the **Basic Action**, which governs everything each character does throughout the **Episode**.

Basic Actions

Hamlet's **Basic Action**: to use madness as a cover while I find out if Claudius is guilty or not.

The **Basic Action** of all the other characters (Reynaldo and the Norwegian Ambassadors excepted): to discover the cause of Hamlet's madness.

Again, we need a clear guideline. Individual **Facts** only have meaning as part of a sequence, between what comes before and what comes after.

Episode 6 is divided into the following **Facts**:

1. Polonius reveals himself as an intriguer and a spy.
2. Ophelia tells Polonius of Hamlet's madness. He concludes love is the cause.
3. Claudius welcomes Rosencrantz and Guildenstern, who have been summoned from Wittenberg to try and discover the cause of Hamlet's strange behaviour.
4. Polonius informs the king he knows the cause of Hamlet's

madness.
5. Claudius receives the Norwegian Ambassadors.
6. Polonius informs the King that Hamlet has gone mad for love of Ophelia whom he has been forbidden to see because Polonius fears she may lose her virginity. He stakes his life on it.
7. Polonius attempts to question Hamlet.
8. Rosencrantz and Guildenstern attempt to question Hamlet.
9. Polonius announces the arrival of the Players.
10. The Players perform for Hamlet.
11. Hamlet reflects on his lack of resolution.
12. Rosencrantz and Guildenstern admit failure to the King.
13. The King and Polonius have arranged a 'chance' meeting between Ophelia and Hamlet, which they will spy on.
14. Hamlet reflects on suicide.
15. Hamlet and Ophelia meet. He realises she is being used and rounds on her.
16. Claudius realises the cause of Hamlet's madness goes deeper and that he is in danger.

Let us now look more closely at **Fact 7**: Polonius attempts to question Hamlet, in which we see Hamlet's strategy in action for the first time.

The **Tasks** for each actor, in line with their **Basic Actions**, are:

Hamlet: I want to use my 'madness' to express my contempt for Polonius.
Polonius: I want to prove my opinion is right (and so save my head).

The Dialogue

POLONIUS How does my good Lord Hamlet?

HAMLET Well, God-'a'-mercy.

POLONIUS Do you know me, my lord?

HAMLET Excellent, excellent well. You're a fishmonger.

POLONIUS Not I, my lord.

HAMLET Then I would you were so honest a man.

POLONIUS Honest, my lord?

HAMLET Ay, sir. To be honest, as this world goes, is to be one man picked out of ten thousand.

POLONIUS That's very true, my lord.

HAMLET For if the sun breed maggots in a dead dog, being a good kissing carrion — Have you a daughter?

POLONIUS I have, my lord.

HAMLET Let her not walk I' th' sun. Conception is a blessing, but not as your daughter may conceive. Friend, look to't.

POLONIUS (*aside*) How say you by that? Still harping on my daughter. Yet he knew me not at first – he said I was a fishmonger. A is far gone, far gone, and truly, in my youth, I suffered much extremity for love, very near this. I'll speak to him again . . . What do you read, my lord?

HAMLET Words, words, words.

POLONIUS What is the matter, my lord?

HAMLET Between who?

POLONIUS I mean the matter you read, my lord.

HAMLET Slanders, sir; for the satirical slave says here that old men have grey beards, that their faces are wrinkled, their eyes purging thick amber or plum-tree gum, and that they have a plentiful lack of wit, together with most weak hams. All which, sir, though I most powerfully and potently believe, yet I hold it not honesty to have it thus set down; for you yourself, sir, should be as old as I am – if, like a crab, you could go backward.

POLONIUS (*aside*) Though this be madness, yet there is method in't. – Will you walk out of the air, my lord?

HAMLET Into my grave.

POLONIUS Indeed, that is out o' th' air. (*Aside.*) How pregnant sometimes his replies are! A happiness that often madness hits on, which reason and sanity could not so prosperously be delivered of. I will leave him, and suddenly contrive the means of meeting between him and my daughter. – My lord, I will take my leave of you.

HAMLET You cannot, sir, take from me anything that I will more willingly part withal – except my life, my life, my life.

POLONIUS (*going*) Fare you well, my lord.

HAMLET These tedious old fools!

Actions

In his effort to appear mad, Hamlet uses obscure words and phrases and a great deal of wordplay. He baffles the other characters, wrong-foots them, teases their minds with statements that are apparently incoherent but which, they suspect, have a hidden meaning, a coded message. His words are the **Actions** he uses both to accomplish his **Basic Action** and to fulfil his immediate **Task**.

We need to go through the scene carefully and look at the language at three levels:

1. The literal sense of the words spoken, the surface text.
2. The deeper, real meaning of the words spoken, the **Subtext**.
3. The way in which one word, one image leads to another, forming a sequence of ideas, a coded message.

For this, we need to consult a good annotated edition† and go through the notes carefully.

The expressions that need to be examined are in italics in the above text. They fall into three groups.

Group One

Fishmonger.

Why fishmonger? Why not a butcher? A carpenter? In the popular language of the time fish = sex. In *Measure for Measure*, when Claudio is condemned to death for having illicit sex, his crime is described by a friend as 'fishing for trout in unusual waters'. There was also a common belief that fishmongers' daughters were particularly fertile and bred easily.

Honest.

This could mean 'upstanding' but could also mean 'chaste' when applied to women. Hamlet moves from Polonius' 'honesty' (probity) to Ophelia's 'honesty' (chastity). Later, 'honesty' means 'proper behaviour'.

Walk i' th' sun.

† The Arden edition (Routledge, London, 1982) can be recommended.

Women of the nobility were supposed to be pale, not sunburned like peasants. Sex was also referred to as 'country matters'. Here the expression means 'lose her virginity'. The sun was a symbol for the king and therefore she should be kept away from him.

For if the sun breed maggots in a dead dog, being a good kissing carrion . . .

The sun's warmth appears to breed maggots and a dead dog is a good breeding ground. But 'carrion' has a secondary meaning: a source of easy sexual pleasure. Hamlet uses the word 'kissing'. Claudius (the sun) is kissing and corrupting Hamlet's mother who has fallen all too quickly into his bed. He is also corrupting the kingdom. Hamlet has already said, 'There's something rotten in the state of Denmark,' ' 'Tis an unweeded garden that grows to seed; things rank and gross in nature [the king and his mother] possess it merely.'

The first part of the coded message starts to emerge from these images all of which are concerned with animal lust, breeding and corruption: Denmark has become a country in which virtue is dead and vice and sexual licence thrive and Polonius is at the heart of the corruption.

Group Two

For you yourself, sir, should be as old as I am – if, like a crab, you could go backward.

As people grow old they progress towards 'second childhood', thus, as Polonius ages bodily he becomes more and more like a child and would at one point be the same age as Hamlet. Later in the play (Act II, scene ii), Hamlet describes Polonius as a 'great baby . . . not yet out of his swaddling clothes', to which Rosencrantz replies, 'They say that an old man is twice a child.'

The second part of the coded message is that Polonius is decrepit and stupid.

Group Three
There are also simple plays on words...

Matter.
Polonius means subject-matter, the content of the book.
Hamlet interprets it as a problem, the subject of a quarrel.

Will you walk out of the air, my lord?
Fresh air was supposed to be bad for people who were ill.
Hamlet takes it to mean dying.

Take my leave.
A set expression but Hamlet interprets the word 'take'
physically, as taking an object, or indeed, his life.

Social and Historical Factors
Our earlier research has revealed a set of social assumptions
which we must make our own, if we are to enter into the
characters' minds:

1. For a young noblewoman to lose her virginity was a
   disgrace for the whole family. Sex for pure pleasure was a
   matter for the lower orders. People of 'good' family
   married within their class, and for reasons of income,
   status, property and inheritance. Virginity was therefore
   essential if the family line was to be unquestionable.
2. Polonius, however high his position at court, is inferior to
   Hamlet, a prince, and so is Ophelia, who, therefore, at
   least as far as Polonius is concerned, is not eligible to
   marry Hamlet. Hamlet will make a state marriage. In
   pursuing his investigation, Polonius must proceed with
   discretion and deference. He may not argue or contradict.
   This makes him vulnerable to Hamlet's barbs. He is
   bound by etiquette and unable to fight back no matter
   what the humiliation.

Hamlet exploits both Polonius' fears for Ophelia's virginity and
his subservient position.

Making the Words Our Own
This textual and background study must become part of our
lived experience. We don't act 'literature' or style or literary

images. We can't play, nor is the audience interested in glossaries and footnotes. If they were, they would stay at home and read the text, not pay to come and watch us. We have to feel and experience all the images – maggots, dead dog – so that they become physical experiences for us, and we use free association and **Emotion Memory** to strengthen and deepen our responses.

These experiences must become part of the **Subtext** that has been worked out earlier in rehearsal.

Similarly, the complexities of actually delivering the written words must be mastered, so that this language, for us actors, becomes our normal language for the duration of the play, not strange words someone else has written.

We cannot consciously motivate the individual images, or supervise the way we deliver the lines, any more than we consciously motivate our legs when moving across the stage. We must concentrate on the **Tasks**:

- I want to use my 'madness' to express my contempt for Polonius to his face.
- I want to prove my opinion is right.

When we do that, everything else falls into place.

We can set out our findings on this scene, as with *Late Love*, in columns, as shown on the opposite page, only this time the **Subtext** is not spoken, only Shakespeare's dialogue. We need to note, however, that in this scene, as often in Shakespeare and classic plays, the asides are the **Subtext**, thoughts spoken aloud.

Tempo-rhythm

Hamlet's outer **Tempo-rhythm** is a walking pace. In musical terms *andante* or *andantino*. (*Andante* in Italian means walking.)

His inner **Tempo-rhythm** is much more excited (*agitato*).

Polonius's outer **Tempo-rhythm** is comparatively faster. He has to run after Hamlet. His inner **Tempo-rhythm** is calm, steady because of his smugness and self-satisfaction.

HAMLET ACTION	SUBTEXT	TEXT	POLONIUS SUBTEXT	ACTION
I come in reading and pretend not to see him.	– Spying as usual. If only he were as clever as he thinks he is.	POLONIUS *How does my good Lord Hamlet?* HAMLET *Well, God-a-mercy*	I must be tactful and not offend him.	I bow respectfully.
		POLONIUS *Do you know me, my lord?*	I must engage his attention.	I follow him.
I keep moving, paying him no attention.	– You are no better than a pimp.	HAMLET *Excellent, excellent well. You are a fishmonger.*		
	I will tell him he's a crook but will do it as though impart- ing wisdom.	POLONIUS *Not I, my lord.* HAMLET *Then I would you were so honest a man.* POLONIUS *Honest, my lord?*	Mad! He has known me since he was a child. Me? Honest? Of course!	
I look at him for the first time.	– Like Horatio.	HAMLET *Ay, sir. To be honest, as this world goes, is to be one man picked out of ten thousand.* POLONIUS *That's very true, my lord.*	I have always taught my children the virtue of honesty.	
	– The King corrupted and seduced my 'honest' mother.	HAMLET *For if the sun breed maggots in a dead dog, being a good kissing carrion —*		
	– You thought I wanted to corrupt your honest daugh- ter, that I am like the King.	*Have you a daughter?* POLONIUS *I have, my lord.*		
	I want to play on his fears.	HAMLET *Let her not walk i'th' sun. Conception is a blessing, but not as your daughter may conceive, friend, look to't.*		
I walk away, reading.		POLONIUS *How say you by that?* (aside) *Still harping on my daughter. Yet he knew me not at first —' a said I was a fishmonger.' A is far gone, far gone, and truly, in my youth I suffered much extrem- ity for love, very near this. I'll speak to him again. — What do you read, my lord?*	[Aside is Subtext.]	

I stop and show him the book.		HAMLET *Words, words, words.* POLONIUS *What is the matter, my lord?*		
I look around for other people.	I deliberately misunderstand him again.	HAMLET *Between who?* POLONIUS *I mean the matter that you read, my lord.*		
I advance towards him, marking every point. I stop.	I invent the contents of the book so I can insult him to his face.	HAMLET *Slanders, sir; for the satirical rogue says here that old men have grey beards; that their faces are wrinkled; their eyes purging thick amber or plum-tree gum; and that they have a plentiful lack of wit, together with most weak hams. All which, sir, though I most powerfully and potently believe, yet I hold it not honesty to have it thus set down; for you yourself, sir, should be as old as I am — if, like a crab, you could go backward.* POLONIUS (aside) *Though this be madness, yet there is method in't.* — *Will you walk out of the air, my lord?*	– Is he dangerous? [Aside is Subtext.]	I step backwards as he advances. I stop.
	– Die?	HAMLET *Into my grave.* POLONIUS *Indeed, that is out o'th' air. (Aside.) How pregnant sometimes his replies are! A happiness that often madness hits on, which reason and sanity could not so prosperously be delivered of. I will leave him, and suddenly contrive the means of meeting between him and my daughter. — My lord, I will take my leave of you.*	[Aside is Subtext.]	
I walk away.	I play on his words. – I wish I were dead.	HAMLET *You cannot, sir, take from me anything that I will more willingly part withal — except my life, except my life, except my life.* POLONIUS (going) *Fare you well, my lord.* HAMLET *These tedious old fools!*	I must find the King.	I bow and go.

PHASE THREE

In Phase Three, this scene becomes part of the total structure. It is placed within the total context, put 'into perspective'. What is the emotional level of the scene? How does it compare with a similar scene, later on, when Hamlet asks Rosencrantz and Guildenstern to play a recorder and then rounds angrily on them? The scenes have a similar structure. Hamlet teases and provokes and then reveals his true thoughts, but whereas in the scene with Polonius he only expresses his feelings after Polonius has gone ('These tedious old fools!'), he lets Rosencrantz and Guildenstern feel the full force of his anger face to face.

All the individual scenes, all the exploratory work, all the actors' contributions are now integrated into the total concept conceived by the director, the costume, set, lighting and sound designers, but at the heart of the performance is the creative actor whose task, as a human being, is to convey the experience of the play to other human beings.

In the final stages of rehearsal, it is useful for actors to go back to the beginning of the rehearsal process and recall the impression that was made on them by their first private reading, and then their feeling of the play as a whole when they discussed it with each other and tried to summarise it as fully and concisely as possible.

If work has been rigorous, precise and logical, and the progress of the rehearsals has been organic, the audience will receive something like the same impression. For them, a performance is rather like a first reading. They take the play in as a whole, as a total experience. The seed that was planted in the actors when they first encountered the play will be the seed that is planted in them.

PREPARATION TIME

As an actor I have to prepare for a performance. Some way has to be found of leaving my daily life, with all its problems and concerns, behind. I must clear my mind of everything other than the play; my voice and body must be working well.

One method of getting into the world of the play is to take

selected, perhaps quite brief moments, and thinking them through, recalling the **Tasks**, checking the sequence of **Actions** they provoke. A mistake is to try and go through the whole play and experience it in my mind. If I do that, I will have given the performance in the dressing-room and there will be nothing left for the stage. All I need is a reminder, a gentle push towards curtain up.

I may be called on to perform the same play several times a week, sometimes over several months, or even years. This presents the problem of keeping the performance fresh and spontaneous. The temptation is to imitate previous performances, to try to play the emotion, or the feeling – the result of action rather than the action itself. In so doing I may simply fall into cliché, or become frustrated because I have tried to take a short cut and the emotion refuses to 'come'. It is essential to play the situation, the cause, each time and allow the emotion to arise through organic processes.

One means of keeping a role fresh is to use the preparation time to test out parts of the role that I feel have become tired and introduce a small new factor into the performance, a small **Task**, or find something relevant but new in my **Emotion Memory**. This will be quite minor and private, and should not affect the overall shape of the performance, or disturb the other actors, but it will bring a dead moment alive.

PART FOUR

Stanislavski's Master Classes on *Hamlet*

By the spring of 1937, the students were sufficiently advanced in their studies to be able to start work on plays. Stanislavski was now very ill and his contribution to the Studio was to review work which his assistants had prepared with the students in a series of master classes.† Much of the work centred on *Hamlet*. A woman student had elected to study Hamlet. Stanislavski approved on the grounds that this emphasised the need to work from one's own self. She would not role-play a man, but use her own life experience for the character.

MASTER CLASS ONE, 21 APRIL 1937 ACT I, SCENE II

The students were in Phase One of the rehearsal process, defining the **Episodes** and **Facts** and their **Basic Actions** and **Tasks** within them, exploring their own **Emotion Memory**.

Preliminary Work

'Hamlet' had prepared an analysis of the scene.

Episode 1. The usurper King tries to win over Hamlet and the court and eagerly occupies the throne.

    Fact 1. The King sends ambassadors to Norway.

    Fact 2. The King endeavours to win the affection and loyalty

---

† These classes were recorded both in the notes the participants took, reproduced by Novitskaya, op. cit., pp. 182–209, and in the shorthand notes that were always taken at Stanislavski's rehearsals and classes, printed in *Stanislavskij Rpetiruet*, op. cit., pp. 492–581. The accounts given here are a conflation of both sources.

of each and everyone: **a**. the King is attentive towards Laertes; **b**. the King ingratiates himself with Hamlet.
Fact 3. Hamlet wants to know what has happened.

Episode 2. Having learned about his father's ghost from his friends, Hamlet decides to solve the mystery.
Fact 1. The meeting of two friends.
Fact 2. Horatio and his friends reveal the secret of the ghost's appearance.
Fact 3. Hamlet decides, come what may, to encounter the ghost.

'Hamlet', 'Gertrude' and 'Claudius' had written out their **Before-time**, up to the death of Hamlet's father.

Discussion in the session centred round the essential difference between **Action**, which has to be precisely planned, and **Adaptation**, which needs to be left free.

Stanislavski first worked with 'Hamlet' and asked her to read her sequence of actions for the scene.

The Class

'Hamlet' [reads]. I have come back home after the death of my father. I remember him, how good it was to be with him. I go to his chair and stroke it. I try to imagine what life will be without him. I try to imagine my mother's grief. But I see her and she is happy. I'm amazed that this could be so. I know who my new father is; I think about it. I try to understand how my mother could have remarried so soon. I watch her, I am distressed.
Stanislavski: You realise you have given actions, and adaptations, and feelings and the situation. But we need something much, much simpler. What is your task in this scene?
'Hamlet': To understand.
Stanislavski: Good, I need to *understand, observe* . . . How would you do that in these circumstances? Here's your concrete situation: I have been away for some time. Now I am back and see that everything has changed. My father is dead, my mother has remarried. You discover a new woman in your mother, she is happy, flirtatious. What would you do in that case?

'Hamlet': I would ask my mother the reason for such a change.
Stanislavski: All right, but you can't talk to your mother, so what do you do then?
'Hamlet': I watch her.
Stanislavski: So, write down these actions: 'to watch'. Does the word 'watch' contain one or many actions?
Students: Many.
Stanislavski: Then break down this action into its constituent parts. Art doesn't deal in generalities; art is always concrete. What would you do to understand the metamorphosis your mother has undergone? I'm moving you out of the actor's world into the real world of human beings. Explain to me what you would do, on the basis of your own human experience, to understand what has happened to your mother. Tell me what you need to do in order to respond to my question. What is going on in your mind, what process?
'Hamlet': Bewilderment. I don't understand what is happening to Hamlet's mother.
Stanislavski: Hamlet doesn't exist, there's no one but you! Relate everything to yourself. Can you imagine, for example, that your neighbour is your mother?
'Hamlet': Could I imagine my own mother?
Stanislavski: All right, let it be your own mother. Use your **Emotion Memory**. What do you need to do to understand the situation?
'Hamlet': I observe my mother, to try and understand why she is behaving in this way.
Stanislavski: And?! Imagine: you come back expecting to see your mother all sadness and tears and instead you find her happy, and what is more, married to a cheap crook. So, choose the person in your own life you find the most repulsive and set him beside your mother. What would you do then?
'Hamlet': I would be jealous.
Stanislavski: So, sit there and be jealous. Can you do that?
'Hamlet': No, I can't.
Stanislavski: Jealousy is the result of many actions. What is your inner process when you see your mother?
['Hamlet' thinks.]

Student 1: I need to strengthen the image of my mother using **Emotion Memory**. What was she like before?

[Stanislavski says nothing.]

Student 2: My mother has changed: she is completely different, I feel her attitude towards me is different.

[Stanislavski says nothing.]

Student 3: I look at my mother and see she has changed. I look at the king and compare him [to my father].

Stanislavski: You're all talking to me in terms of results but I want you to talk to me in terms of actions. Go on.

'Hamlet': I remember my mother. She was so loving! The way she gave my father his tea, how attentive she was towards him.

Stanislavski: You have individual pictures, individual images. Now, using your **Emotion Memory**, paint a large picture for me, with a tender mother who loves you and her husband, imagine the bedroom and then . . . quite a different picture: you see your mother married to an absolute blackguard! She is happy and contented.

'Hamlet': It's all very sketchy.

Stanislavski: It mustn't be sketchy. You must clearly imagine your whole life from your childhood to the death of your father. How can we put that together? It is a combination of individual **Emotion Memories**, tiny episodes you are particularly fond of. String all these facts together and weave a life out of them. Create a picture out of detailed images of everything that is dear to you. But this picture musn't be sketchy. You must have a deep, precise knowledge of your whole life. This is priceless material which will serve you in your future roles. You should be collecting it throughout your life. The first condition of art is the following: once I have been given a role, say, Hamlet, thereafter there is no difference between Hamlet and me. I exist in Hamlet's situation. Take everything from your **Emotion Memory**.

'Hamlet': Do I have to imagine that I have been studying in Wittenberg?

Stanislavski: Of course you've been studying! And picture to yourself the institution where you've been studying. Perhaps you have an idea what Wittenberg looks like? Something perhaps totally imaginary which only has meaning for you? Then use it! If I dictate your line to you, I'll only confuse you, and I want you to take everything from your own **Emotion Memory**. I don't want to impose anything.

Student 3: But what if, when I have performed all the actions, and start to superimpose the text on them, I find it doesn't match.

Stanislavski: You know the nature of an action, its structure. Once you know it you can perform it in any situation, in any adaptation. For example, you know the truth and logic of getting dressed, it's part of you. Imagine you have performed this action thoroughly, have studied it and you say to me. 'Now I will play it for you.' I have a free day, there's no rush, I get up and start to get dressed. The process is so familiar I do it unconsciously. So, your thoughts come freely. Then you change the situation: 'Today I'm late for class and so I have to hurry.' I have to perform all the actions involved in dressing, without missing one of them, in five minutes. The next phase could be panic. Tell me: do you all understand? If not, say so.

A Student: In our first year you said that an actor needs to know *what* he is doing but not *how* he is doing it. But when I wrote out my physical actions, I wrote out *how* I do them.

Stanislavski: Why write out the how? That will change each time, it will be new, different. And that's good. All great works of art have logic of feeling. As we approach a role we find feelings, a world and physical actions we know. And we see that the physical actions tally with the text almost in the same sequence. I look for the role in you, and I ask you to do the simplest things so that you can understand the logic of a given character. [To 'Hamlet'.] So, what will I do to understand my mother's behaviour?

Assistant: The hardest thing for them is to behave as themselves. When the students are sitting there, thinking, I have the feeling they are somehow doing it as someone else, not as themselves.

Stanislavski: In life, do you find it hard to behave as yourself?

'Polonius': Yes, but do I really do that? In my mind I create a sort of second self and I see how this person behaves. He moves about, says hello to people, someone asks him about something; but, at the same time, I know it's me.

Stanislavski: So you copy yourself? Avoid that like the plague. All you will get are clichés. Copying is not art. Always do everything as yourself, ask yourself, 'What would I do today if I were in this or that situation?'

Student 3: There are physical actions and adaptations?

Stanislavski: There is physical action as such and there is physical action that requires adaptations. Never preplan your adaptations – that's a trick, it's cliché. Be careful not to let adaptations become ends in themselves. [To 'Hamlet'.] What worries you about Hamlet? You have to compare your mother, what she was and what she is? Where are the physical actions? Comparing is *physical action*, albeit *in the mind*. Our creative process is to be inventive both in our own role and the play. There is action in mental images, and these *inner actions* are *physical actions* because they provide the *impulse*, the *urge* to physical action. You need to stir these *impulses*. *Impulses* are the pointer to action. If actions are preplanned, contrived, we end up with clichés.

A Student: I would like to be sure we are doing things right. Let's imagine, I go to see my fiancée's parents to see whether she is still my fiancée or not, and walk into a quarrel. What should I note, that I open the door, look at the room, enter, close the door, turn my head this way and that?

Stanislavski: No, don't fix turning your head, but the fact that you walk into a quarrel, an unexpected squabble but that you pretend not to notice, that's what you should fix. Let's say you are tidying a room. Whatever the circumstances, there are certain actions you have to perform and they will always be the same.

'Hamlet': But surely, if I tidy my own table, dust it and put everything on it in order, then I'll do it one way, but if it was my dead mother's table, and I remember her fondly, I'll do it differently, won't I?

Stanislavski: The actions will always be the same. It can't be otherwise. You will dust and tidy the things but your attitude to them will be different.

'Hamlet': And how do we express that attitude?

Stanislavski: Perform the actions in the given circumstances and don't think the feelings they should be evoking. Do them properly, logically, as you would do them today in your present mood, and study present circumstances in all their complexity. When you act in the present you don't notice how your feelings arise.

'Claudius': Yes, but what am I supposed to write down in my notebook? Will one person do one thing and someone else another?

Stanislavski: That notebook is meant only for you! If I take it I won't understand a word of it because I have my own book which matches my own personality. Remember, the most important thing is to create the impulse to action in an actor.

'Claudius': My task is, *to know whether I am acceptable or not?*

Stanislavski: That is your *task*, your *action*.

'Claudius': I would like to read you my sequence of physical actions in the coronation scene, to see if I have got it right. [He reads his notes, which include some adaptations.]

Stanislavski: Not bad, but all I would call actions is:

1. I test out attitudes towards me.
2. I hold on to the queen for her authority.
3. I hide my feelings from Hamlet.

These are all actions.

But I avoid Hamlet's eyes, I watch him when he is not looking at me, I smile lovingly at him when he is talking to his mother – these are *adaptations*. There is no need to set them.

'Gertrude' [reads her sequence of actions]: My new, beloved husband and I are in the throne room of our castle. With us are Hamlet, Polonius, Laertes, Lords Voltimand and Cornelius, whom the King is sending to Norway as ambassadors, to come to a settlement with him about the conduct of his nephew. I support the king in this. My **Basic Action** is, *I want to present my new husband in such a way that he will be accepted.* I look at all present, I smile at him, lovingly gaze into his eyes, fawn on him. The King is talking to Laertes, promising to grant his request, his dearest wish. I nod to express my agreement with the King's words. Puzzled by Hamlet's mood, throughout the scene I look at him affectionately, encouragingly, and so try to lift his dark mood and reconcile him to his uncle – his new father. I try to persuade him to stop grieving for his dead father, death is everyone's lot. I ask him to stay at home and not return to Wittenberg.

Stanislavski: There's far too much there – adaptations, the circumstances etc. *Your main task* is to *present your husband in such a way that he is accepted.*

'Gertrude': Yes, but I have to do something to make sure that happens.

Stanislavski: What would you do, then – I mean you personally?

'Gertrude': Look at everyone, perhaps smile.

Stanislavski: You're still giving me adaptations but what I want from you are actions. *To present your husband.* That action contains many smaller actions. To make sure he is accepted you might have, perhaps, to *fawn, cajole* and *bribe*, and all these actions require adaptations, those you have mentioned and others. Can you sense how rich the whole score is? Do all that and you have fulfilled your task.

Assistant: Could I sum up everything that has been done and said today so we can incorporate what we have learned into the 'system'?

Stanislavski: That's a good idea, it will consolidate what we have been doing.

Assistant: In every scene we look for *the basic action for each character*, which results in *action*, for example, in Hamlet's case, *to understand*. This major action, in turn is broken down into smaller actions, for example: *I observe, I compare my mother then to my mother now* etc. We reveal these actions using an infinite number of adaptations. *For the Queen, the basic task, the action to be performed, is 'to present my husband in such a way that he is accepted'.* This major action is broken down into smaller actions – to *fawn, cajole, bribe*. These, in turn, produce adaptations: to calm Hamlet, take someone's chin, give someone an affectionate look etc. *We only set physical actions, large and small.* There is no need to set our adaptations, they should emerge anew, every day.

Stanislavski: Absolutely right.

MASTER CLASS TWO: ACT I SCENE III

A room in Polonius' apartments. Laertes' departure.
[The students are in Phase Two and are beginning to use the written text.] Stanislavski's concern in this class was to establish the sequence of **Organic Actions**.

The Class

The students outlined the content of the scene:

Laertes, who is about to embark for France, takes leave of his sister, asks her to write to him and urges her to keep away from Hamlet, not to trust in his love. Perhaps he loves her now but because of his high estate he cannot make good his words of love:

> . . . his will is not his own,
> For he himself is subject to his birth.
> He may not, as unvalued persons do,
> Carve for himself . . .

And so he begs her to be cautious because:

> Virtue itself scapes not calumnious strokes.

Ophelia promises to heed his words, but she, in turn, asks him not to lead too joyful a life, not to be an empty barrel. Polonius enters. He tells Laertes to make haste:

> The wind sits on the shoulder of your sail.

He gives Laertes a long list of advice, to hold his tongue, not to be familiar with just anyone, to dress richly but not vulgarly, neither to lend or borrow money. Laertes takes his leave. There is further talk between Polonius and Ophelia about Hamlet and their relationship. Ophelia tells her father of Hamlet's love, his vows, his behaviour towards her. Polonius forbids her to meet or speak to Hamlet again, and demands she return his gifts. Ophelia agrees. She will obey her father's will.

Stanislavski: You followed the text, the situation as it develops, but I want you to find the sequence of organic actions.

'Ophelia': Organic actions?

Stanislavski: The process is always the same. If you like, start with contact. First of all you must find organic actions and basic contact.

'Ophelia': But actions alter according to circumstance.

Stanislavski: No, organic actions are always constant in all circumstances but, depending on the situation, one will be darker, another will, on the other hand, be brighter, clearer. So, what is Polonius doing in the scene with Ophelia?

Assistant: **Fact 3**: *Polonius, following on from what Laertes has said, demands that Ophelia tell him of her past relationship with Hamlet and keeps her apart from him.*

'Polonius': In this **Fact**, I get the truth out of her about her relations with Hamlet, I insist, I prevail upon her.

Stanislavski: So, to compel and persuade her, you have to look at her. You need to know who Ophelia is, observe her closely.

'Polonius': I know her very well.

Stanislavski: Do you have a daughter called Ophelia? Did Shakespeare?

'Polonius': If she were my daughter, I would try to persuade her, prevail upon her, even command her.

Stanislavski: What do you mean by persuade? You would probe her with your eyes, sound her out thoroughly, try to find out what she is like today. [To 'Ophelia'.] Remember, this depends also on you. If he wants to sound you out, you want to do the same to him.

'Polonius': I don't want her to see what I'm thinking.

Stanislavski: But you do want to know what's happening to her, even if you want to hide the fact from her. So, you want to persuade her. What does *persuade* mean? What is the human process of *persuading*? You need *mental images,* so that not only you, but also your fellow actor can see what you see. You must not persuade 'in general'. You need to know the purpose for which you are persuading – your goal.

'Polonius': We established my *creative task: to warn her off Hamlet, to forbid all further meetings and conversations.*

Stanislavski: Yes, I agree. And you, Ophelia?

'Ophelia': My *creative task is: while I try and justify myself and Hamlet,*

I want to submit to my father's will. Can I ask you a question? As Ophelia, I make my entrance near the end of Act I and important events have occurred before that. Do I have to go through all that from the very beginning? Later, I'm off-stage again for a long time, and when I do appear I am mad. It's a difficult transition.

Stanislavski: You have to use your imagination to create the transitions. It is essential to pull all the individual moments of the role together.

'Ophelia': Shakespeare makes me admit to my father that I love Hamlet, but personally, I wouldn't do that.

Stanislavski: To admit you are in love to your father is very difficult. If you have to speak to save Hamlet, that is difficult, too, but you steel yourself and do it. But you're running ahead of yourself. All I want you to do is find an organic sequence. It finally comes down to contact. To perform organic actions you need all the elements of your psychotechnique: focus, imagination, logic and sequence, muscular release, since while you are tense, you cannot communicate.

'Polonius': But if I ask you a question and am extremely impatient for an answer, I go tense but still communicate.

Stanislavski: Not so. In that instance, you won't be tense but concentrating hard. You need a task and a sense of truth and belief, **Emotion Memory**, and, once there is contact, adaptations. Before you can start to speak, you have to adapt to your fellow actor. What else?

'Polonius': Once I have understood what mood, what state of mind my daughter is in, I have to tell her why I have come.

Stanislavski: So, you *turn towards her, sound her out, capture her attention,* then, *convey your mental images to her. You verify* how she has taken them. You need to know the situation. You have to use your imagination to create mental images.

'Laertes': Why is it that every time I walk on stage everything I have worked out seems to vanish?

Stanislavski: Because the fact of appearing in public tempts you into self-display. All I'm asking you to do is perform a sequence of actions simply and logically, but if you do that just to please the audience, then you become its slave. An axiom: the audience does not exist. Never have contact with them. It requires enormous technique not to notice them.

FINAL MASTER CLASS, 13 JUNE 1938: ACT I, SCENE II

This was probably Stanislavski's last class before his death some two months later.

He was working again on Act I, scene ii of *Hamlet*. The students were well advanced into Phase Two.

'Hamlet' had experienced great difficulty with the soliloquy, 'O that this too, too solid flesh'. Stanislavski's first concern was to find Hamlet's **Basic Action/Task** in the opening scenes of the play and only to allow the actor to play that specific **Task**, that 'now' moment, and not to be influenced by **Fact/Events** which occur later in the play. In this way, the soliloquy becomes an **Action**, part of the fulfilment of the **Task**.

In their discussions, he and the actor also defined the **Supertask**: discovering the meaning of existence.†

Stanislavski later turned to the general problem of speaking Shakespeare's text, rather than partly improvised dialogue, and the technical difficulties involved.

The Class

Stanislavski: You see the King and Queen. He is on the throne, she is happy. What would you do if you were Hamlet? Get into that mood.

'Hamlet': I would try to understand, ask questions, mostly of myself, I have to look into this matter, why it has happened.

Stanislavski: Then do it. You couldn't do anything with the soliloquy because you'd acted the whole play already. Before you can hate you must understand – simply find out where you

---

† This was the **Supertask** Stanislavski defined for his production of *Hamlet* in 1911, on which he collaborated with Gordon Craig. Both men took a quasi-religious view of the play. This **Supertask** differs from the one we used in the exercise in Part Three.

are; how am I to live, where can I go? It takes him a great deal of the play to understand. But, for the moment, all you know is that your father is dead, and your mother has married your uncle. You have to come to terms with that, take it on board, and inwardly digest it. But you knew the whole play from the very start. And you played this scene knowing everything that happened, so there was nothing left for you to do, the play was over. That is illogical. You were illogical and played what doesn't yet exist.

'Hamlet': In the scene on the platform with the ghost, all I have to do is understand?

Stanislavski: Yes, the ghost appears. You have to learn, understand, test, in fact do *everything possible, to learn and understand everything* you have been denied.

'Hamlet': The ghost reveals the meaning of life, the earth and the hereafter.

Stanislavski: That is *knowledge of events*. You have discovered the **Supertask**.

'Hamlet': I begin to establish where my father is, I revolt against his being in Hell.

Stanislavski: No. Hamlet will only talk about that a month or two after he has seen the ghost. For the moment, you are dealing with a phenomenon you can't grasp. You merely take it in, listen to the ghost, whom you still don't recognise but sense. You must be terribly careful not to offend the ghost.

'Hamlet': I understand that my father is telling me to take revenge, but how?

Stanislavski: If you already knew what you are going to do for the next four acts, what would you have left to play? Your **Task** is to *take in everything he says*, then work it out. Another thing: you mustn't talk to the ghost in the way you did. You must speak quietly, not move your arms, so as not to frighten it.

'Hamlet': I can't form a picture of the ghost – is he big or small? I can't get the feel of him and yet I'm supposed to be terrified of him.

Stanislavski: You want to know what your feelings are and set them? That's impossible. That's like saying, I have to experience terror. You may experience it, you may not. Whatever the ghost may be like, the first thing you have to do is ask, 'What would I do if . . .'

'Ghost': How do I become ethereal, how do I turn into a ghost?

Stanislavski: The ghost is a flickering presence. You can't approach it. [To 'Hamlet'.] The action here is very simple – *finding out*. Hamlet still cannot draw a clear line of action out of this encounter because he has doubts. The tragedy of Hamlet is that he has undertaken an impossible task. You try to understand the secret, you meet the ghost, and after you have, you are still where you started. You know nothing, understand nothing. You have to start from the very beginning. That begins a new act, a new life, there is matter here for reflection. You go on living but in a different situation. When Rozencrantz and Polonius come to Hamlet, he cannot understand how they can live in a world of trivia after he has learned a terrifying secret, which has brought something tremendous into his world. That is what the tragedy is about. He cannot take anything of the daily round to his heart because he knows something greater, more meaningful. Concentrate on the fact that he becomes excited and has a moment of self-realisation when a human being (the actor performing the speech on Hecuba) weeps passionately over someone else's fate, feels it, experiences it. Hamlet begins to understand that he can do things that previously seemed *impossible*. *Hamlet is purposefulness*, first of thought, then of action. Do we now have to discuss how to do Hamlet?

Assistant: Please.

Stanislavski: Hamlet knows nothing, understands nothing, he cannot see how his mother accepted his father's death and married again:

> . . . and yet within a month –
> Let me not think on't. Frailty, thy name is woman! –
> [A little month], or ere those shoes were old
> With which she followed my poor father's body,
> Like Niobe, all tears, [why she, even she] –
> O God! a beast that wants discourse of reason
> Would have mourned longer – married with mine uncle.†

† The words in square brackets are omitted in the Russian translation.

He cannot accept his uncle as king or as his mother's husband. He has to *discover the truth*. Enter Horatio: 'Horatio or I do forget myself.' He wants to know how he is, *why he is here*. 'What make you from Wittenberg, Horatio?'

And suddenly the news: 'Methinks I saw him yesternight.' *He has to digest this tremendous news*. Then the encounter with his father. He tries to learn everything his father can tell him. Hamlet learns that his uncle killed his father. His father demands revenge! How? Remember the scene with the oath: 'The time is out of joint, O cursed spite that I was ever born to put it right.' What is Hamlet's **Supertask**?

Students: Man in conflict with life.

Stanislavski: That's the content. We talked about the **Supertask** earlier – *understanding existence* i.e. *to discover the secret of life*.

'Claudius': Could we go back to scene ii, the second **Fact**, the King sends ambassadors to Norway. I find that kind of official act difficult, I become false.

Stanislavski: Sending ambassadors is a very common act.

'Claudius': But we do it during a magnificent coronation.

Stanislavski: As you are already on the throne, it cannot but be magnificent. But magnificence is not what it's about. The scene has great political significance; you are sending emissaries from your own country to another. You can't sit on the throne and 'pick your teeth'. You have far too little authority, you need much more. It's very important to find the right rhythm. It must arise from the situation. The wrong rhythm can make you handle the situation wrongly. You can go to your coronation jumping for joy or as though you were in a funeral procession. But, in any case, today, I didn't understand 90 per cent of what you said because of all the false stress. There were individual words but no sentences. What's difficult about this play? The fact that you can't afford to miss a single word. The most important thing in this play is human thought and if one word goes wrong it means there is a missing link. But with you, the whole thought was missing. Your diction is poor. No diction, no phrasing. Do you realise how important they are in a play like this? When you were using your own words, they conveyed the meaning very well. But today I didn't understand a thing, because as soon as you began to use the text, you forgot about verbal action and so became false. What do we mean by false? Singsong diction. The first indication of falseness is speaking without seeing anything. If you say, 'Lovely weather' in the same way as you say, 'My heart is full', that is false. Shakespeare is full of great thoughts and you can't speak great thoughts in the same way as you order breakfast. [To 'Hamlet'.] Go through the soliloquy for its thoughts. Try to convey the mental images behind those thoughts.

['Hamlet' is silent.]

Stanislavski: Why don't you say something? What are you doing?

'Hamlet': Trying to concentrate.

Stanislavski: You're looking for feelings? Despite everything you know, you're going to play feelings? Don't do that. Just try to tell me what the thoughts are but express them clearly. Try to convey the images behind these thoughts.

'Hamlet':

O that this too too solid flesh would melt . . .

Stanislavski: I don't understand why you needed to say that. Explain the thought. What does it mean? You are in a hurry, but you must paint a picture for me. What's been happening?

'Hamlet':

O that this too too solid flesh would melt . . . [Pause.]

Stanislavski: No, you really can't stop, not for a second. You really can't break the flow of sound. There must be one continuous note. You don't have any kind of *cantilena*.† The sentence must be delivered as a whole.

'Hamlet':

O that this too too solid flesh would melt,
Thaw, and resolve itself into a dew . . .

Stanislavski: 'Flesh', 'thaw', 'resolve itself into a dew'. It's a vast

---

† A long melodic line usually delivered on a single breath.

canvas. Where are the stresses? You're in a little trouble because you're in a hurry. When you deliver a long sentence you mustn't separate subject and predicate, they must be linked but not run into one another. There must be form.
'Hamlet':

> O that this too too solid flesh would melt,
> Thaw, and resolve itself into a dew . . .

Stanislavski: Why 'thaw'? What does it mean? 'Into a dew' should be the end of the phrase. Shape the next phrase, don't let one run into the other. What are you talking about?
'Hamlet':

> Or that the Everlasting had not fixed
> His canon 'gainst self-slaughter . . .

Stanislavski: Look at the structure of the phrase. There are three nouns, one of them is the subject. The subject-noun is always stressed, you know that! You start to hurry the words 'or that the Everlasting'. That rhythm continues. Do you feel how the phrase develops? Say 'self-slaughter' as though it were something desirable. 'Slaugh-' is the key syllable. Go on from there to the climax 'O God! O God!' All you need to do is heighten it a little. Where's the real difficulty? The fact that you have to speak it well. If your voice has no tone, no resonance, you try to find ways of making it work. That's when all these vocal tricks start. When do you start being false? When the voice isn't working, when it isn't placed. It's a matter of daily exercises. Your main task is technique, technique and more technique. That's very difficult but once you've understood, it becomes easy. Why is it difficult? Because it requires systematic, daily work. You have to do exercises every day. Not only on words but on the whole of your physical apparatus. You need a great deal of fire and energy to overcome the bad impression you make on audiences with badly spoken lines, wooden hands and all the rest. You have to train yourself to control everything – voice, speech, movement etc. You must train at the Studio, at home, every free minute. There's no time to work on your physical apparatus when the show has begun. Now is the moment to develop your technique. We are getting nearer and nearer to the subconscious and the more subtle our work, the better trained our physical apparatus must be to develop it. You mustn't be worried if I criticise you. I've been working on things which we must work on throughout our whole career. *Hamlet* is the most difficult of plays. And I gave it to you. *Hamlet* will make you understand all that high feeling and words require. Is there anything wrong in that? You will discover, you will live *Hamlet*, that greatest of works of art. The work you are doing is difficult, impossible and essential. If you succeed in this work it's as though you had succeeded in a hundred other plays. All the work you have done will stand you in good stead.

Let's sum up: your physical and organic actions are now more or less right. There was no real verbal action but when it did happen it was very good. But we have mainly been concerned with physical action. We've only just started work on verbal action. We have to turn sequences of physical actions and inner impulses into verbal action. When we have done that, we can shape the play.

Conclusion

The 'system' is not a magic formula for success, or an insurance policy against failure. Diligently performing the exercises as some kind of ritual will not turn a bad actor into a good actor. The 'system' is as good as the person who uses it.

It is not a moral obligation either. There is no special virtue in using it. It is a working method for working actors. For those, including, initially, his wife, who could not see the merit in it, Stanislavski had a simple reply, 'If you find it useful, then use it, if you don't, don't.'

What the 'system' can do is provide a means for actors to gain control over their gifts so that they can make the best use of them.

To use the 'system' and the Method of Physical Action as Stanislavski understood them requires time and working conditions that, in the present climate, seem impossibly ideal. They no longer exist, even in Stanislavski's own Moscow Art Theatre. Few companies can afford a year or more's preparation. Six weeks' rehearsal is a luxury today. This means that we have to adapt the Method of Physical Action to fit economic and financial constraints. But actors who are trained in the 'system' have the considerable advantage of knowing how much work they have to do at home, on their own. A coherent working method makes that task much easier.

What, perhaps, is an even greater legacy is what Stanislavski called the actor's 'ethic', the notion that all the technical skills of mind and body only have meaning if put to the service of the play and the audience. While my responsibility as an actor is to develop my own talent and to achieve the highest degree of artistry, I also have to develop a sense of ensemble, a realisation that I depend on other members of the company as they depend on me, and that only together can we create the performance. As Stanislavski put it, 'Leave your ego at the stage door as you come in.'

Appendix One: Variations in Terminology

Just as the 'system' evolved over a period of many years, so did the terminology which Stanislavski used to describe it. The most familiar English terms are those used by Elizabeth Hapgood when translating Stanislavski's *An Actor's Work on Himself, Parts One and Two* (*An Actor Prepares*, 1936, *Building a Character*, 1950). Mrs Hapgood's translation of the terms was questioned soon after Stanislavski's Russian text became available.

The terms used in this book correspond to those Stanislavski actually used in class, not in his books.

In the following diagram, the key terms used at the Studio are

Studio	An Actor's Work on Himself	An Actor Prepares
SUPERTASK *Сверхзадача* Sverkhzadacha	SUPERTASK	SUPEROBJECTIVE
BASIC ACTION Основое действие Osnovoa dejstvie TASK **Задача** Zadacha CREATIVE TASK **Творческая задачаа** Tvorcheskaja zadacha	TASK	OBJECTIVE
EPISODE (EVENT) Эпизод (**Событие**) Epizod (Sobytie) FACT/EVENT **Факт** /(**Событие**) Fakt/Sobytie	BIT (This translates Кусок (Kusok) a term which was not used at the Studio)	UNIT
THROUGH-ACTION **Сквозное действие** Skvoznoe dejstvie	THROUGH-ACTION	THROUGH LINE OF ACTION

in the first column, those Stanislavski used in the Russian edition of his works in the second and the terms Elizabeth Hapgood used in the third.

Mrs Hapgood's terms, 'Unit' and 'Objective', are more abstract, less immediate than the words Stanislavski used which are very much 'hands-on'. The term from *An Actor's Work* translated as Unit is an ordinary word, *kusok*, which means 'bit', 'slice', as in a slice of bread or meat. Similarly, the word translated as Objective, *zadacha*, means two things: an immediate task I have to perform, or a mathematical problem I have to solve. In both cases, it is something I have to do now, not something projected into the future. Stanislavski often talked about an actor's or character's 'Goal', *tsel*, but that is not the same thing as a Task. In Elizabeth Hapgood's translation, moreover, Bit (Unit) and Task (Objective) are sometimes confused.

The main shift in Stanislavski's own usage was in the terms used when breaking down a play. Originally, when drafting his books, he used one word, Bit, but he became aware that there was a danger of breaking the play down into too many tiny fragments and of losing sight of the whole. He then made a distinction between large, medium and small Bits. At the Studio he talked of Episodes (Events, large Bits), Facts/Events (medium and small Bits), terms he had used earlier in his career in his drafts and notes. This was mirrored in the use of the term Basic Action or Creative Task for the Task within the Episode, and Action for what was done in the Facts/Events.

Appendix Two: Index of the Principal Terms Used

Action(s) What is done in order to fulfil a **Task**.

Adaptation The adjustment of behaviour, the changes of strategy required in order to fulfill a **Task** or reach a goal.

After-time The events which occur after the end of the play.

Basic Action A character's main intention in an **Episode**, a major **Task**.

Before-time The events which precede the opening of the play, or each new entrance.

Circle of Attention The area in which concentration is focused.

Dramatic 'I' The person, the character I create in a play that corresponds to a human being in life, a **Real 'I'**.

Dramatic Situation *See* **Given Circumstances**.

Emotion Memory The conscious use of the recall of experiences, either physical or mental, from one's own life, which match the experiences of the character as described by the author.

Episode A coherent sequence of events, forming one of the major segments of the play.

Fact or **Fact/Event** One of the smaller constituent parts of an **Episode**.

Given Circumstances The situation in which characters find themselves in an **Episode** or a **Fact**. These circumstances will ultimately include the director's and the designers' concepts.

Here, Today, Now Being the present, in today's rehearsal, responding to minor changes, or new creative ideas which we and others have brought to our work, not attempting mechanically to reproduce what we did yesterday.

'I am Being' The creative state that arises when the border-line between the actor and the character is blurred.

Inner Monologue The thoughts that are going through our minds while we are speaking dialogue, or listening to others.

Mental Images The pictures we have in our mind, the 'film', when we are speaking or listening.

Necessity The needs, wants which compel us to act in the real world.

Object of Attention The person or thing on which concentration is focused.

Organic Actions Actions or sequences of actions which have their own logic and must be performed in a specific order whatever the situation.

Performance Mode The total state of technical preparedness, physical and mental, which leads to subconscious creative activity and artistic spontaneity.

Perspective/Planning The overall shaping of a play in the late phases of rehearsal, ensuring the placing of climaxes and the comparative intensity of each scene.

Real 'I' Who I am in life.

Subtext The combination of **Inner Monologue** and **Mental Images**, the sum of our mental activity during the dialogue.

Supertask The subject or theme of the play, the end towards which all **Tasks** move.

Task What a character has to do, the problem he has to solve, in a **Fact** to achieve his end.

Tempo-rhythm The basic pace of a scene and the rhythms of the individual actions within the pulse.

The Third Being The actor/role, the product of the marriage between the actor's personality and the character the author has written.

Through-action/Counter-through-action The logic of the sequence of actions, which binds together all the single actions and enables the character to reach his goal.

Through-emotion The logic of the sequence of emotions which run parallel to the actions.

What 'if'. . . The basic question to be asked when trying to establish the reality of a dramatic situation and my part in it. 'What would I do if I were in this situation?'